SHEPHERD'S NOTES

When you need a guide through the Scriptures

Ecclesiastes/ Song of Solomon

BROADMAN
&HOLMAN
PUBLISHERS

Nashville, Tennessee

0–8054–9059–0
Dewey Decimal Classification: 223.8
Subject Heading: BIBLE O.T. ECCLESIASTES
Library of Congress Card Catalog Number: 98–17995

Library of Congress Cataloging-in-Publication Data
Ecclesiastes and Song of Solomon / Duane Garrett, editor
     p. cm. — (Shepherd's notes)
    Includes bibliographical references.
    ISBN 0–8054–9059–0
    1. Bible. O.T. Ecclesiastes—Study and teaching. 2. Bible. O.T. Song of Solomon—Study and teaching. I. Garrett, Duane A. II. Series.
    BS1475.5.E26   1998
    223'.807—dc21

                                  98–17995
                                    CIP

1 2 3 4 5 6   03 02 01 00 99 98

CONTENTS

FOREWORD

Dear Reader:

Shepherd's Notes are designed to give you a quick, step-by-step overview of every book of the Bible. They are not meant to be substitutes for the biblical text; rather, they are study guides intended to help you explore the wisdom of Scripture in personal or group study and to apply that wisdom successfully in your own life.

Shepherd's Notes guide you through the main themes of each book of the Bible and illuminate fascinating details through appropriate commentary and reference notes. Historical and cultural background information brings the Bible into sharper focus.

Six different icons, used throughout the series, call your attention to historical-cultural information, Old Testament and New Testament references, word pictures, unit summaries, and personal application for everyday life.

Whether you are a novice or a veteran at Bible study, I believe you will find *Shepherd's Notes* a resource that will take you to a new level in your mining and applying the riches of Scripture.

In Him,

David R. Shepherd
Editor-in-Chief

DESIGNED FOR THE BUSY USER

Shepherd's Notes for Ecclesiastes and Song of Solomon is designed to provide an easy-to-use tool for getting a quick handle on these significant Bible books, important features, and for gaining an understanding of their messages. Information available in more difficult-to-use reference works has been incorporated into the *Shepherd's Notes* format. This brings you the benefits of many advanced and expensive works packed into one small volume.

Shepherd's Notes are for laymen, pastors, teachers, small-group leaders and participants, as well as the classroom student. Enrich your personal study or quiet time. Shorten your class or small-group preparation time as you gain valuable insights into the truths of God's Word that you can pass along to your students or group members.

DESIGNED FOR QUICK ACCESS

Bible students with time constraints will especially appreciate the timesaving features built into the *Shepherd's Notes*. All features are intended to aid a quick and concise encounter with the heart of the messages of Ecclesiastes and Song of Solomon.

Concise Commentary. Short sections provide quick "snapshots" of the themes of these books, highlighting important points and other information.

Outlined Text. Comprehensive outlines cover the entire text of Ecclesiastes and Song of Solomon. This is a valuable feature for following each book's flow, allowing for a quick, easy way to locate a particular passage.

Shepherd's Notes. These summary statements or capsule thoughts appear at the close of every key section of the narratives. While functioning in part as a quick summary, they also deliver the essence of the message presented in the sections which they cover.

Icons. Various icons in the margin highlight recurring themes in the books of Ecclesiastes and Song of Solomon, aiding in selective searching or tracing of those themes.

Sidebars and Charts. These specially selected features provide additional background information to your study or preparation. Charts offer a quick overview of important subjects. Sidebars include definitions as well as cultural, historical, and biblical insights.

Questions to Guide Your Study. These thought-provoking questions and discussion starters are designed to encourage interaction with the truth and principles of God's Word.

DESIGNED TO WORK FOR YOU

Personal Study. Using the Shepherd's Notes with a passage of Scripture can enlighten your study and take it to a new level. At your fingertips is information that would require searching several volumes to find. In addition, many points of application occur throughout the volume, contributing to personal growth.

Teaching. Outlines frame the text of Ecclesiastes and Song of Solomon, providing a logical presentation of their messages. Capsule thoughts designated as "Shepherd's Notes" provide summary statements for presenting the essence of key points and events. Application icons point out personal application of the messages of the books. Historical Context icons indicate where cultural and historical background information is supplied.

Group Study. Shepherd's Notes can be an excellent companion volume to use for gaining a quick but accurate understanding of the messages of Ecclesiastes and Song of Solomon. Each group member can benefit from having his or her own copy. The *Note's* format accommodates the study of themes throughout Ecclesiastes and Song of Solomon.

Leaders may use its flexible features to prepare for group sessions or use them during group sessions. Questions to guide your study can spark discussion of Ecclesiastes and Song of Solomon's key points and truths to be discovered in these delightful books.

LIST OF MARGIN ICONS USED IN ECCLESIASTES AND SONG OF SOLOMON

 Shepherd's Notes. Placed at the end of each section, a capsule statement provides the reader with the essence of the message of that section.

 Historical Context. To indicate historical information—historical, biographical, cultural—and provide insight on the understanding or interpretation of a passage.

 Old Testament Reference. Used when the writer refers to Old Testament passages or when Old Testament passages illuminate a text.

 New Testament Reference. Used when the writer refers to New Testament passages that are either fulfilled prophecy, an antitype of an Old Testament type, or a New Testament text which in some other way illuminates the passages under discussion.

 Personal Application. Used when the text provides a personal or universal application of truth.

 Word Picture. Indicates that the meaning of a specific word or phrase is illustrated so as to shed light on it.

ECCLESIASTES INTRODUCTION

THE DATE AND AUTHORSHIP OF THE BOOK

Ecclesiastes 1:1 implies that Solomon is the author of Ecclesiastes. This had been the common understanding of the authorship of the book until about two centuries ago, when critical scholars challenged Solomonic authorship. By the beginning of the twentieth century, matters had reached the point that the idea of Solomonic authorship was all but unthinkable and even many conservative scholars came to believe that the book had been written in about the fourth century B.C., long after the time of Solomon. Scholars have argued that the language of the book has the characteristics of late Hebrew, that the content of the book implies that at least two different people had a hand in writing it, that the outlook of the book reflects contact with Greek philosophy, and that Ecclesiastes was not accepted as part of the Hebrew Bible until very late, which indicates that it could not have been written as early as the time of Solomon.

Two Writers Behind Ecclesiastes?

Many interpreters believe that the book indicates that there was a man known only as Qoheleth (Hebrew for "the Teacher" or Ecclesiastes) who wrote a book of pessimistic reflections on the world. His own thoughts are reflected in the book where the text uses first person, as in "so I said" (Eccl. 9:16). These interpreters believe that a second person later edited the book by the Teacher and added his own comments. This editor is sometimes called the

The Language of Ecclesiastes

The Hebrew of the book is unusual. Some scholars have actually argued that it was originally written in another language, although most regard this as unlikely. The book contains a fair number of words that seem to come from Aramaic (a language related to Hebrew), two words that appear to be Persian, and some unusual grammar. On close examination, however, Ecclesiastes does not contain nearly as much Aramaic as scholars once thought, and the Aramaic that does appear in the book does not require a late date. The Persian words are also not nearly as significant as some have argued. These words seem to have entered the common vocabulary of the ancient Near East much earlier than previously thought. The peculiar Hebrew of Ecclesiastes cannot be evidence for a late date since it does not fit anywhere in the known history of the language.

Qoheleth

Qoheleth is Hebrew for "the Teacher."

Ecclesiastes has some conspicuous parallels to Egyptian and Mesopotamian literature that is far older than Greek literature (and earlier than the age of Solomon). In particular, Ecclesiastes 9 is so similar to a section of the ancient epic of Gilgamesh that it is impossible to deny that the author of Ecclesiastes knew this work. Solomon had a reputation for knowing all the wisdom of his day, but would an obscure writer in fourth-century Palestine have had knowledge of this literature? Probably not.

"frame narrator," and his sections are marked by references to the Teacher in the third person (e.g., Eccl. 12:10).

It is better, however, to view the movement between first and third person as a deliberate literary device by a single author than as a sign that two different authors were at work. Sometimes the book is reflective and personal and in the first person; at other times it takes a more distant, "objective" stance and uses third person. At times it sounds like the voice of Wisdom, giving its lessons in traditional proverb form. Ecclesiastes is a masterpiece, and its shifting of perspectives should not be regarded as the result of clumsy editing but as a literary strategy.

Greek Philosophy in Ecclesiastes?

Some scholars urge that Ecclesiastes shows a dependence on Greek thought and literature, which again would imply that it was written long after Solomon. Many interpreters compare Ecclesiastes to the cynic, Epicurean, and stoic traditions in Greek philosophy. None of this is very convincing, however. Nothing in Ecclesiastes has any clear connection to Greek literature beyond the most superficial resemblance.

Questions of Canonicity

Many scholars argue that the rabbis were still arguing about whether the book of Ecclesiastes should be included in the Hebrew Bible as late as the first century A.D. If true, it is hard to imagine how the book could have been written by Solomon. Surely the canonical status of a Solomonic book would have been settled long before the beginning of the rabbinical period. Here too, however, the argument is not really compelling. There is little doubt that the book was understood to be canonical by the rabbis. There may well have been some debates about it (the book does seem to be very pessimistic). But ancient rabbinical debate does not invalidate the canonicity of the book any more than modern scholarly debate does. It is a simple fact that Ecclesiastes is a troubling book, and people are bound to debate about it.

- *In summary, nothing in the book demands*
- *that we hold to a late date for the book. In*
- *contrast, the book itself, as well as some of its*
- *incidental details, points to Solomonic*
- *authorship. We should note, however, that*
- *he writes under the pen name "the Teacher"*
- *(or Qoheleth). Out of respect for the designation which Solomon gives himself, we should*
- *use the same term.*

The Message of Ecclesiastes

Ecclesiastes has attracted an amazing diversity of interpretations. It would be fair to say that today no single reading of the book prevails. Instead, there are many schools of interpretation.

A Work of Evangelism

Among conservative Christians, it is traditional to read Ecclesiastes as a kind of evangelistic book that aims to show that devotion to God is the only path to happiness. It shows that all the other ways of attempting to find happiness are futile. Thus, when the Teacher says that everything is "meaningless" (1:2), he means that everything is meaningless for the person who does not know God. There is some truth in this interpretation, but it is superficial and works

Canonicity

Paul House says, "Canonical books . . . are God-given documents that people of faith feel constrained to obey. Such books differ from other religious texts for these reasons, rather than for any literary or historical brilliance they may display." Thus, each of the 66 books of the Bible are said to be canonical or part of the Christian canon.

3

In the final analysis, Ecclesiastes does drive the reader to the fear of God, but it does so in the process of a far more complex argument than this analysis indicates.

well with only a few passages. For example, it is easy to say that the Teacher is pointing out that life without God is empty in 2:1–11, but what about 3:18–22? At various points, taking Ecclesiastes as a simple evangelistic tract is forced. Furthermore, the thematic statement that all is "meaningless" seems to be an absolute statement and not a description of the unhappiness of the unbeliever—something that can be easily changed by becoming a believer.

Dour Pessimism

At the opposite extreme is the view that Ecclesiastes is the work of a bitter and cynical pessimist. In this interpretation, the Teacher looks at the world as an enigma with no discernible purpose or direction. God knows what will be, but humans cannot know. We are left to grope in the dark. Injustice is everywhere and death annihilates all. The best we can do is try to enjoy life, forget the pain, and forget our questions.

It is not hard to find passages that seem to validate this interpretation, but the interpreter must also treat quite a bit of the book as later, secondary additions by a more pious editor (the "frame narrator") in order to achieve consistency. In other words, taking Ecclesiastes as a work of cynicism will not work well unless the interpreter removes passages that speak more positively of the fear of God. The Teacher's faith in the justice and goodness of God runs deep in this book (see 8:12–13; 11:9).

An Existentialist Tract

In a thoroughly modern reading of Ecclesiastes, some scholars say that the book denies that existence is rational. Nevertheless, the book affirms that existence itself is a good thing and exhorts the reader to turn to inner experience as the one domain of freedom and meaningful existence. Like a good existentialist, the Teacher asserts that even though the world is meaningless, we can create meaning for ourselves by persevering in the quest.

This is in many respects a severe misinterpretation of the book. The Teacher has no interest in validating his own existence simply by acting out his self-made ideals. He never says something like, "Even though I know that the quest for wisdom is futile, I am going to keep on doing it anyway because it is the quest itself, however hopeless it may be, that gives me purpose." To the contrary, he considers a hopeless quest for truth to be a bitter, life-consuming activity (1:13–18). In reality, the Teacher tells us to orient our lives to the fear of God and in that context to find pleasure in the tasks which life has for us.

Reflection on the Fall and Human Mortality

Any meaningful approach to Ecclesiastes must begin by asking two questions. First, for whom was this book originally written? Second, does Ecclesiastes interact with any other body of literature or school of thought?

It is clear that Ecclesiastes was written for the educated elite in the ancient Near Eastern setting. It is addressed, in short, to a male aristocracy known as the "wise." The implied readers were people who were likely to have access to the king and to the circles of power. For these people the pursuit of wealth was a real possibility and not just a fantasy. They had the leisure time for intellectual pursuits. The author of Ecclesiastes spoke to men who knew about traditional wisdom, warning them of the limitations of human wisdom. His original readers were wealthy people, or at least people who could aspire to wealth, and he warned them of the folly of the pursuit of money while advising them on how to maintain reasonable income.

These people would have known about the Babylonian and Egyptian skeptical philosophy, and they would have been troubled themselves by the serious questions raised by this literature. The Teacher responded that although life is often arbitrary, despair and cynicism are not appropriate responses. People should enjoy the good things life offers and yet maintain reverence for God.

This brings us to the answer to the second question. It is obvious that the Teacher wrestled with the apparent futility of life. What is not so obvious is that the early chapters of Genesis constitute the crucial text for coming to grips with this problem. In Genesis, Adam—the lord of humanity and wisest of men—fell into sin and became subject to miserable toil and death. The relationship between man and woman was broken, and humanity was cast away from God, where they vainly struggled for knowledge, wealth, and power. What they really longed for was eternal life (not just endless existence but a sense of permanent value), but they were cut off from the tree of life. The presentation of God as an absent and hidden God in Ecclesiastes arises directly from Gen. 3, where the man and woman are sent out of the garden.

Thus, Ecclesiastes teaches us how to live in the world as it really is. Its primary message is simple: *You are mortal.* Recognition of our personal mortality leads to three conclusions:

First, this life and all we do with it is passing away. All things are fleeting, and thus nothing

Vanity

The frequent refrain that all is "meaningless" is a play on the name of Abel, the murdered son of Adam. In Hebrew, the word translated "vanity" is the same word as the Hebrew form of the name *Abel* (*heel*).

has real, lasting value. All our accomplishments, passions, creations, and desires will pass away.

Ecclesiastes is an ancient book written in an ancient way. Like a number of Egyptian books of wisdom, it approaches its subject matter by going to and fro among several topics. In Ecclesiastes, these topics include wisdom, wealth, political power, death, and religion. But even as it moves about in a seemingly random manner, it is driving us toward its major conclusions regarding the nature of this life and the fear of God.

Second, life should be enjoyed for what it is. Pleasure is not the point of life, but one should not miss the fleeting joys which life affords. This is not hedonism or cynicism. It is not a way of saying that life is meaningless and absurd and we might as well just party and enjoy ourselves. But it is a claim that our days under the sun are very few, and we should not waste them in toil and vexation.

Third, and most important, we must revere God. If we are mortal and He is God, then we should fear Him. It is only by accepting the truth about what we are and about who God is that we can find peace.

OUTLINE

The book of Ecclesiastes is different than modern books. It contains a logical presentation of content, featuring several main points with subpoints.

ECCLESIASTES MAY BE OUTLINED AS FOLLOWS:

Title
(1:1)

On Time and the World
(1:2–11)

On Wisdom
(1:12–18)

On Wealth
(2:1–11)

On Wisdom
(2:12–17)

On Wealth
(2:18–26)

On Time and the World
(3:1–15b)

On Politics
(3:15c–17)

On Death
(3:18–22)

On Politics
(4:1–3)

On Wealth
(4:4–8)

On Friendship
(4:9–12)

On Politics
(4:13–16)

On Religion
(5:1–7)

On Politics
(5:8–9)

On Wealth
(5:10–6:6)

Transition
(6:7–9)

On Wisdom and
Death (6:10–7:4)

Transition
(7:5–6)

On Wisdom and
Politics
(7:7–9)

Transition
(7:10)

On Wisdom and Wealth
(7:11–14)

On Virtue and Sin
(7:15–29)

Transition
(8:1)

On Politics
(8:2–6)

Transition
(8:7–8)

On Theodicy
(8:9—9:1)

Transition
(9:2)

On Death and
Contentment
(9:3–10)

Transition
(9:11–12)

On Politics
(9:13–10:17)

Transition
(10:18–20)

On Wealth
(11:1–6)

On Death and
Contentment
(11:7–12:7)

Conclusion
(12:8–14)

QUESTIONS TO GUIDE YOUR STUDY

1. Summarize the arguments for and against Solomon's authorship of Ecclesiastes.
2. What is the meaning of the word *vanity* as it is used in Ecclesiastes?
3. What are the key themes of Ecclesiastes?

ECCLESIASTES COMMENTARY

TITLE (1:1)

Most translations call the author of this book the "Preacher" or "Teacher." The Hebrew word used here (*Qoheleth*) is difficult to interpret, but it seems to mean a person who convenes an assembly for the purpose of teaching. Because of the uncertainty about this word, many scholars and translators simply use the Hebrew word *Qoheleth* to refer to this book and its author. The Teacher tells us that he was "Son of David, king in Jerusalem," a description that could fit any member of the Davidic dynasty from Solomon down to the fall of Jerusalem in 586 B.C. In 1:12, however, the Teacher states that he was king "over Israel."

ON TIME AND THE WORLD (1:2–11)

Whether we translate the first word of verse 2 as "vanity" or as "meaningless," the text seems to imply deep pessimism about the value of life and the world.

It would be wrong to picture the Teacher as a dour, humorless cynic who hated life and saw none of the goodness of creation. Such an evaluation would describe human life in the world after the Fall and apart from God's grace. In this condition, we live brief and painful lives, and we are confronted every day with death and the transitory nature of life.

The first three chapters of Genesis actually give us both sides of creation and the human condition. On the one hand, all of creation is "good" and a work of God (Gen. 1). In creation, the glory and power of God are made visible for all

The text claims that its author was a son of David and king over all Israel. Only Solomon fits this description. After the death of Solomon, his son Rehoboam succeeded him as king. The people took this opportunity to complain that Solomon had driven them too hard, forcing them to work as virtual slaves on his building projects. The older advisers counseled Rehoboam to pay attention to the people's complaints and give them relief, but his friends told him to let the people know who was boss by coming back with a harsh, inflexible position. He took the advice of his friends but soon regretted it. The people rebelled, chose Jeroboam as their leader, and formed an independent, northern kingdom (don't be confused by the names; Jeroboam was not related to Rehoboam nor was he of the line of David; he had been an official in Solomon's government). Therefore, only Solomon was both son of David and king in Jerusalem over all Israel.

to see (Ps. 19:1–6; Rom. 1:19–20). Even in their fallen condition, men and women continue to marvel at the craftsmanship of God. On the other hand, we are now a lost people. The children of disobedient parents, we continue to suffer the bewilderment of facing life without God, the guilt and estrangement that comes from being sinners, the anguish of marital and family discord, the drudgery of toiling in a world that seems to fight against us every step of the way, and the terrifying indignity of death itself—a power that nullifies all that we are (Gen. 3:6–24).

Ecclesiastes focuses on Gen. 3 rather than Gen. 1, and it explores all the areas of human sorrow that Genesis refers to. It tells the reader that its focus is on the story of the Fall by calling everything vanity or *heel*. The Hebrew word *heel*, is pronounced like *Abel*, the name of Adam's murdered son. As the victim of Cain's jealousy, Abel/*heel* represents humanity's sorrow and predicament.

In verses 3–7, the Teacher compares the human condition to that of the world itself. On the one hand, the lifetime of a person, compared to the age of the earth, is very brief. Generations come and go, but the earth remains "forever." In this case, "forever" does not mean literally that this planet has existed and will exist for all eternity, but that compared to the earth, the life of a person is but a passing moment—*heel*. Knowledge of how short-lived we are compared to the world contributes to our sorrow and vexation.

On the other hand, the world, too, seems trapped in vanity. The sun, seeming like a perpetual motion machine, goes around and around (v. 5). As the sun moves eternally from

Vanity

The Hebrew word *heel* actually means "breath" or "vapor," and thus it comes to mean "transitory" and hence "worthless," like the English word *vapid*. As a one-word description of the world, it seems to contradict God's one-word evaluation of the world—that it is "good" (Gen. 1:31).

Ecclesiastes frequently looks back to the early chapters of Genesis, but it gives much more attention to the Fall in Gen. 3 than to creation in Gen. 1. This accounts for the pessimistic tone of the book.

east to west, so the wind circles eternally from north to south (v. 6).

The forces of creation seem monotonous and ineffectual. The same is true of verse 7, which describes the rivers as always flowing into the sea but never raising the sea level by a single inch. Some translations take the end of verse 7 to mean that the streams go back to the place from which they came, as though the text were describing the water cycle. This is not the correct translation, and scientific analysis is again not the point of the text. The Hebrew means that the rivers *continually* flow to the place toward which they go. An unceasing work is seen to be ineffectual: Rivers constantly pour water into the ocean but fail to raise the water level. This is a parable for human life; it is unceasing labor that has no permanent results.

The translation of verse 8 is much disputed, but one reasonable interpretation is:

A   All things are weary.

B1   No one is able to speak,

B2   the eye is not satisfied by seeing,

B3   and the ear is not filled with hearing.

In the Hebrew text, the lines here designated B1, B2, and B3 have exactly the same grammatical structure, so that they parallel one another. Line A describes everything as "weary," a term that suits the condition of unceasing, fruitless labor described above. The sun, for example, huffs and puffs like a runner endlessly circling a track. The three lines B1, B2, and B3 describe the human response to the world. We cannot "speak" means that we cannot make sense of the world; it comes to us as a fact and we cannot

In studying the Old Testament, avoid reading modern ideas and scientific concepts into the text. Otherwise, we make the Old Testament say something it does not and miss its point. When verse 5 says that the sun runs across the sky, it is not trying to tell us anything about astronomy. The point here is not to give a scientific description of natural history, but to present a human and even subjective view of the movements of these forces.

The point is that none of this satisfies us. We crave more, but we do not know what. Something is missing.

really *explain* it. Also, we can never have enough of seeing or hearing, similar to how the rivers never can fill the sea.

The lament of verses 9–10, that there is nothing new under the sun, moves the train of thought to the next level. If all things continue without ceasing, then a person can safely say that nothing really new ever appears. We cannot overturn this argument by appealing to new technology and inventions, things such as televisions and airplanes, as though these kinds of things were the Teacher's concern. He is really speaking of the human condition, a condition that is defined by weakness, ignorance, and finally by death itself.

Technology cannot change this, not even the utopian scenarios proposed by the more optimistic varieties of science fiction. Technological innovations may provide a measure of comfort and ease, and they can also create fresh crises, but they are not germane to the discussion of Ecclesiastes except that they provide another failed attempt to bring into being the "new" thing that will save us from anxiety and sorrow. We might set ideology and "new" political philosophies alongside technology in this regard.

Systems ranging from libertarianism, to communism, to racist fascism all claim to have discovered a "truth" that will liberate humanity from blindness, suffering, and emptiness. All fail, and most only make the situation worse. Today, at least in the West, most people hold to a kind of democratic principle with a modified capitalism. They do this not out of a conviction that these are powerful new philosophies but that they are practical means that allow us to muddle through a difficult and confusing life.

These ideals will not save us, and they are not really new. If the Teacher could survey modern society and examine the "advances" since the Enlightenment, he would have no reason to change his verdict that nothing is new.

In verse 11, the Teacher says that in addition to there being nothing "new," no one is remembered in the days after his death. Here again, the fact that some people have achieved lasting fame does not refute this verse. At most, these people might be the exceptions that prove the rule (compared to the few names long remembered, how many hundreds of millions have passed on in anonymous obscurity?). But even these most famous of people do not contradict the rule. Continuing to emphasize human mortality, the Teacher makes the point that fame does not transcend human mortality. Those famous people whom we sometimes call the "immortals" of history were in fact very mortal. Although their names may be remembered, the people themselves are for the most part forgotten. Time moves on, and everyone drowns in its wake.

The New Testament answers the longing of Ecclesiastes. It has the "new" things that bring true and eternal value into human life.

But there is one thing that is "new" after all. It is remarkable how often we encounter the adjective "new" in reading the New Testament. First and foremost, Christ gives us a new covenant (Luke 22:20). Jesus' teaching is new wine that requires new wineskins (Luke 5:37–38). Jesus gave the church a new commandment (John 13:34). Even pagans, when they heard the apostles, were amazed at the "new" teaching (Acts 17:19). In Christ, we live a new life in the Spirit (Rom. 7:6). We enter this by means of the new birth (1 Pet. 1:3). Anyone in Christ is a new creation— indeed, everything is new (2 Cor. 5:17). The saints in glory sing a new song (Rev. 14:3) as they await the culmination of all things, the new heaven and the new earth (Rev. 21:1). None of this contradicts Ecclesiastes. To the contrary, it fulfills the longing of Ecclesiastes.

■ *Humans are mortal, and all that they accom-*
■ *plish is fleeting. They long for some new*
■ *thing that will answer their questions and*
■ *meet their needs. Our only hope is in the One*
■ *who came down from heaven as God's Son.*

QUESTIONS TO GUIDE YOUR STUDY

1. What is the meaning of *quoheleth?*
2. What does it mean to say that there is nothing new under the sun?

Remembered

To be "remembered" is to achieve a kind of immortality, in that one's name lives forever in the minds of people. Even today, people speak of an athlete, artist, or statesman "achieving immortality." The Teacher declares that this is illusory.

In the context of ancient wisdom literature, *wisdom* does not strictly connote a profound understanding of life and the ability to give advice to people, although that is part of wisdom. For ancient peoples, "wisdom" included specific skills—such as artistic skills, intellectual achievements, the amassing of facts, and even the ability to interpret dreams and omens. Not all "wise" people were necessarily good.

3. What are the implications of the fact that people aren't remembered long after their death?

4. Are people like Julius Caesar, Shakespeare, and Mozart exceptions to the claim that people are forgotten after their death?

ON WISDOM (1:12–18)

In this section, the Teacher gives his first statement on wisdom. His assessment is surprisingly negative.

The acquisition of knowledge and wisdom is treated as the noblest of all tasks in philosophic and wisdom literature throughout the world. Chinese Confucianism considered the scholar to be the supreme position to which a gentleman could aspire, and ancient Egyptian literature said the same thing about the scribes, the learned class of that culture. Plato held up the ideal of the philosopher. Even in Judea, the scribes were a kind of intellectual aristocracy that found itself standing in opposition to a young rabbi from Nazareth named Jesus. For the court of Solomon and for Solomon himself, acquiring knowledge and understanding was the privilege and calling of kings and their courtiers.

But the task of acquiring knowledge, according to the Teacher, was a futile undertaking. It was seen to be not a high privilege but a "heavy burden," a phrase that really means "lousy job." In verse 15, he describes it with a proverb: "What is twisted cannot be straightened; what is lacking cannot be counted." A metal rod that has been bent can never be made truly straight again; in the same way, some problems cannot be solved. The quest for perfect knowledge only ends in failure. Some problems are simply beyond us, and there are many things that we simply do not know. Furthermore, the Teacher also found that chasing knowledge only brought sorrow. The truth about the world is sometimes bitter, and not all discoveries are happy and pleasant.

- ■ *The attempt to find meaning in life through*
- ■ *the acquisition of knowledge is futile because*
- ■ *the task itself is full of frustration and*
- ■ *because knowledge often leads to more pain*
- ■ *and disillusion.*

ON WEALTH (2:1–11)

At the opposite extreme from trying to attain a meaningful life through wisdom is trying to find fulfillment through money and the pleasures that it buys. Actually, however, the two are not so far apart. One person tries to overcome the futility of life by acquiring knowledge, and another tries to deal with the same problems by accumulating wealth. Both are futile. Pleasures, like the quest for knowledge, are meaningless.

The Teacher will deal with wealth several times in Ecclesiastes. Here, he focused on the pleasures that money can buy. In later texts he will talk about different aspects of wealth.

In 2:1, the Teacher emphasized that he began the exploration of pleasure as a deliberate decision to see if it would satisfy him. In verse 2 he tells us that it did not. Sometimes the Old Testament (and Ecclesiastes in particular) will state its conclusion in advance, at the very beginning of a discussion, and then work through the process of coming to that conclusion. This kind of advance notice is called "proleptic." He found that the pursuit of pleasure was "mad," that is, that people who live for pleasures are self-deceptive and very foolish. It is important to note that he did not mean that laughter as such is evil; rather, trying to party as hard as possible as a means to dealing with our mortality is madness. There is a kind of enjoyment of life that the Teacher will recommend, but first it is important to see that pleasures as such do not remove the sting of death.

He began his inventory of pleasures with wine, but added the note that his mind was still guiding him (v. 3). This is important, because it means that he did not become an alcoholic, mindlessly obsessed with liquor. No one needs to be told that a debauched, wasted person has somehow missed the meaning of life. The point is that he indulged in wine and other pleasures and yet retained self-control.

But the Teacher did not simply drink wine. He also built great houses, parks, and vineyards for himself. It would be a mistake at this point to concern oneself over the question of whether having these things is evil in itself. The question before the reader is not "Is it wrong to be rich?" but "Can the benefits of having money bring meaning to this short life?" The answer again is no.

In the same way, although both slavery and concubinage are morally wrong, the text is not concerned with moral issues. It focuses on the question of whether wealth delivers a person from the fundamental human condition. The Teacher describes himself as having all the assets that marked an ancient man as super rich. He had large herds and flocks, silver and gold, slaves, concubines, estates, and farms. His conclusion was that all this is vanity (*heel*). It is fleeting, it does not satisfy, and it did not render him any less vulnerable to death.

- *The pleasures that money can buy do not*
- *deliver us from our mortality. People who*
- *live in fear of personal oblivion cannot fill*
- *their emptiness through indulgence.*

ON WISDOM (2:12–17)

Once again, the Teacher turned to the subject of wisdom. Here, however, the principal issue is not whether true knowledge is accessible to humans (which is the main issue in 1:12–18) but whether wisdom is any real advantage over folly.

The translation of the second half of verse 12 is debated among scholars; most try to change the text to have it mean something like this: "What can a person do who comes after the king? Only what is already done." The Hebrew literally says, "For what can the person do who comes after the king whom they have already made?" Also, the word translated "the person" is literally "the *adam*," using the same word that also means "Adam."

Although the meaning of this line is open to dispute, one reasonable suggestion is that it refers not just to King Solomon, but to the original king of humanity: Adam. In this text, perhaps Adam was called "the king" for three possible reasons: (1) because he was the first lord of the human race, (2) because calling Adam "the king" establishes a connection between him and King Solomon, and (3) because it would be

The Teacher had singers in residence. Singers were the principal form of entertainment in the ancient world of his time. Modern analogies would be a home entertainment system and luxury box seats in a sports arena.

The Teacher did something that was almost unthinkable in the wisdom tradition of the ancient world: He compared wisdom with folly in order to determine whether one was better than the other. The very idea that wisdom may not be vastly superior would have been considered blasphemous to this school of thought.

confusing to call him simply Adam because the Hebrew word *adam* had already been used with the meaning "person" in this verse. Understanding the "king" here to refer to Adam explains the odd phrase, "whom they have already made." This refers to the creation of Adam/humanity, an event first mentioned in Gen. 1:26, where God spoke of Himself in the *plural* ("let *us* make man").

The point of the line is this: Is anyone likely to come along who is wiser than Adam—the one who came directly from the hand of God and who was given the task of naming all the animals (Gen. 2:19–20)? No. Yet Adam's wisdom did him no good, and in the end he perished and returned to the dust (Gen. 3:19). Solomon's wisdom and our wisdom give us no advantage over the ignorant and foolish, because all people alike die and return to dust.

The Teacher affirmed that wisdom is a good thing because at least the wise understand what is happening to them while fools understand nothing (2:13–14). But in the end, wisdom fails because the wise and the foolish both die (2:15–17). One should recall that "foolish" here does not mean those who are stupid; it refers to those who deliberately turn from wisdom in their pride and evil desires.

We can understand the Teacher's point if we think of it in these terms: One person lives a prudent life. He loves reading and learning; he avoids vices and self-destructive habits; he always wears his seatbelt when driving and avoids high-fat foods. Another person is self-centered, self-indulgent, cuts corners whenever he can, takes advantage of others, drinks and smokes heavily, and is sexually profligate. We may assume that the first man will live longer than the second. But we do not know this for certain, and at any rate both men will definitely die. The Teacher sees clearly the absurdity of this.

■ *Wisdom and learning are certainly better*
■ *than recklessness and foolishness. Neverthe-*
■ *less, the advantage is clouded by the univer-*
■ *sal fact of death. If the wisest of people have*
■ *been brought down by death, so will every*
■ *human being.*

ON WEALTH (2:18–26)

In the previous text on wealth (2:1–11), the Teacher described his experience with the luxury that money can buy and his discovery that it does not meet the fundamental needs of humans. This text looks at wealth from the standpoint of how difficult it is to acquire it over against how quickly it disappears. The main point here is that we can be certain that we will lose all the money and things we have so painfully acquired.

The key word is "toil" in verse 18. It reminds us of the curse on Adam, that only through hard labor would he be able to eat of the fruit of the ground (Gen. 3:17–18). The Teacher spoke of his life of acquiring knowledge and things as burdensome, as difficult as the toil of the peasant. He admitted that his high position did not give him immunity from the common ills of the human race. He despaired (v. 20) when he realized that all his gardens, palaces, and gold did him no good in the face of death. The obvious point was that he would not be able to take his riches with him beyond the grave, but there was more to it than that.

In the ultimate sense, a "privileged" life has no privilege at all. It, too, is filled with labors, and those labors are made all the more absurd by the fact that the abundant wages he has received vanish away as he himself returns to dust. Indeed, the industrious person of wealth suffers an indignity that the person of modest means never experiences. Those who have acquired vast wealth through intelligence and determination know that it will pass some day into the hands of those who have done nothing to earn it and who may well squander it.

When verse 24 says that there is "nothing better" than that we should eat, drink, and enjoy life, it does not mean that we should embrace hedonism, or the pursuit of pleasure. Rather, the point is that joyful acceptance of the good things this life has to offer is both right and important. This verse concerns the fleeting pleasures that a person can find in this world. Obviously, the reader who uses this verse as an excuse to play rather than pray or to sleep rather than serve is taking the text out of context and using it as an excuse for selfishness. But we should not miss the point of this verse, either. A life of bleak austerity, a life that has no hearty laughter, is a waste of the few days under the sun that God has given us.

This led to a general observation that all people lead lives of toil and hardship and that in the end they have nothing to show for it (vv. 22–23). This, in turn, moved the Teacher to his first assertion that a person should enjoy the fleeting days of life under the sun (v. 24). This is in keeping with the message of the whole book: We are mortal. We and all that is of this world are fleeting; all is *heel*. But this does not mean we should live in bleak despondency. Rather, because our days are few under the sun, we ought to enjoy them.

The ability to enjoy life is itself a gift of God. Ecclesiastes briefly mentions the third ramification of human mortality—that we should fear God. Those who know God—those to whom He is pleased to give His gifts—can truly enjoy the bounty that even a world of *heel* has to offer (v. 26). Those who do not please Him can anticipate a life of heaping up possessions but never really enjoying them.

■ *Whether a person is rich or poor, life is full*
■ *of toil. Everything a person gains through a*
■ *life of labor vanishes at death. We must rec-*
■ *ognize the good things for what they*
■ *are—fleeting—and we should enjoy them*
■ *while we live. The capacity to do this is a gift*
■ *from God.*

ON TIME AND THE WORLD (3:1–15b)

This is the most widely celebrated passage in Ecclesiastes. It is beautiful in its simplicity, but its simplicity is misleading. What does it really mean to say that there is a time to sew and a time to tear? The "surface" meaning, that sometimes you sew cloth together and sometimes you tear it apart, is obvious. But the *significance* of this observation is not apparent, and readers have pondered these words and wondered about their meaning.

Common interpretations, such as the notion that the Teacher is presenting a "cyclical" view of time, seem alien to the world of this book. A cyclical view of time is the idea that events occur over and over again and that history is not moving toward a goal. By contrast, a "linear" view of time claims that history is moving from a beginning to an end.

The Teacher's actual message is both simpler and more profound. With his declaration that there is a time to kill and a time to heal, or a time to build and a time to tear down, he asserted that *we humans are creatures of time*. The appropriateness of an action is often determined by time and circumstance. We would always like to do the positive things. To build, to laugh, and to sing are the kinds of activities we feel good about. It is harder to see the good in destroying a building, weeping, or saying farewell. But each is appropriate in its season, and our lives are governed by those seasons.

When a person is a baby, it is appropriate to crawl; when he grows older, it is not appropriate. There is a time when it is right to plant a garden (in the spring). But in the fall it is right to pull up plants. Neither action is inherently good or bad, but either can be bad or foolish in certain circumstances.

This text is in two parts. The first, verses 1–8, is a wisdom poem on the subject of time and mortality. The second part, verses 9–15b, comments on the meaning of the poem. Verse 15 is

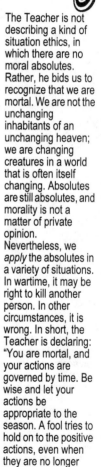

The Teacher is not describing a kind of situation ethics, in which there are no moral absolutes. Rather, he bids us to recognize that we are mortal. We are not the unchanging inhabitants of an unchanging heaven; we are changing creatures in a world that is often itself changing. Absolutes are still absolutes, and morality is not a matter of private opinion. Nevertheless, we *apply* the absolutes in a variety of situations. In wartime, it may be right to kill another person. In other circumstances, it is wrong. In short, the Teacher is declaring: "You are mortal, and your actions are governed by time. Be wise and let your actions be appropriate to the season. A fool tries to hold on to the positive actions, even when they are no longer appropriate."

in three parts, here called a, b, and c; a and b go with this section, but part c is actually part of the next section.

Verse 1 makes the main point that all the following verses will illustrate: Human life is governed by "seasons" for which there are appropriate activities. This verse looks back to Gen. 1:14, in which God created the heavenly bodies to govern times and seasons.

Although almost all translations render the opening line of verse 2 as, "a time to be born," the Hebrew actually says, "A time to give birth." The English seems more logical, but the Hebrew describes what the Teacher is actually trying to say. As the second half of verse 2 indicates, the focus is on giving new life (planting) and ceasing to give new life (uprooting). As we pass through our days, there is a time when it is right for us to bring new life into the world, and there is a time when it is appropriate for us to die. The former seems better than the latter, but each has its place, and we should not resist or deny this reality.

Death, destruction, and mourning are fundamental aspects of our existence, and we need to get used to the idea. On the other hand, healing, building, and laughter each has its place as well, and we should not miss them. Wisdom enables us to know the proper time for each.

Verses 3 and 4 contrast activities that we naturally regard as positive (healing, building, laughing, and dancing) with activities that we think of as negative or bad (killing, tearing down, weeping, and mourning). The important point, again, is that each of these activities has its place in this world of impermanence. Although killing is generally wrong, in some cases it is necessary. The wanton destruction of a building, such as that done by vandals, is a terrible and disgusting thing, but there are times when older structures must make way for the new. We are again creatures who must deal with time and circumstance. Later in Ecclesiastes, the

Teacher declares that funerals and times of mourning are beneficial because they force us to confront the facts of our mortality (7:2).

What does the Teacher mean by "gathering" and "scattering" stones in verse 5? It could refer to clearing a field for plowing ("gathering stones") versus scattering stones in the field of an enemy—something armies would do in order to ruin the economy of a territory they had invaded. Or, "gathering stones" could refer to preparation for building a wall or a house, but it is not clear why one would "scatter" stones. It is probably important that the second half of the verse describes "embracing" and refraining from doing the same since context is usually our best guide in the interpretation of a line. This implies that the expression about the "stones" is a euphemism.

Verse 7 reminds us of the importance of recognizing the proper time for each act. To speak when one should be silent or to be silent when one should speak reflects lack of wisdom and maturity. Just like physical cloth, the fabric of life involves both sewing and ripping, and we should know when each action is appropriate.

Verse 8 mentions the greatest antipathies of all: love and hate, war and peace. Yet each has its place. "Hate" in this context does not refer to a mental state of bitterness, irrational antagonism, or an unforgiving spirit. It describes opposition to an idea or action. The important point is that each of these has its place in life. We must know when to oppose and when to support. It is not realistic to expect that perfect harmony will be attained in this world. The desire for perfection can lead to an attitude that is too quick to compromise and too slow to confront. On the other

Scattering and gathering stones

The early rabbis taught that scattering and gathering stones was a euphemistic way of describing being sexually active versus being sexually abstinent. In light of context, this is probably the best interpretation. Within marriage, an active sexual life is good and necessary. Outside of marriage, it is wrong. People speak of wanting their love to go on "forever." As an expression of commitment to love one another and be faithful unto death, this is a good thing. But even marriage comes under the domain of death and, like the rest of human existence, is fleeting.

Verse 6 speaks to the human desire to make this life and the things of this world permanent. We must recognize that we cannot hoard the things of our mortal existence. Trying to keep everything is another way of refusing to deal with the transient nature of life.

hand, a person must know when confrontation is to be avoided. There is a proper season for each activity.

In verses 9–15b, the Teacher tells us what conclusions he draws from the above poem. In light of the fact that we are mortal and that all we do is governed by time, verse 9 has profound meaning. To say that the laborer gains nothing from his toil is to say that human activity is nullified by death. We are trapped in time, and the fruits of our labor vanish as we pass out of time.

Thus, life is a great "burden" that God has laid on people—it has been laid upon them in the sense that God pronounced a curse upon Adam that his life would consist of hard labor until the time of death (Gen. 3:17–19). More than that, however, people are caught in an unbearable tension. Like the animals, they are bound by time, and everything is beautiful and good at the right time. On the other hand, unlike the animals, the human race has a longing for eternity. We yearn for it, but we do not possess it. We grope after it, but we do not comprehend it. With one foot in time and one in eternity, people find it difficult to maintain their balance.

There is, of course, something glorious about the fact that humans have eternity in their hearts (v. 11). The wonder of being human is that we need God. Without Him we are lost, confused, and prone to corruption. But our yearning for eternity is a good thing. This a part of what it means to be made in God's image.

The Teacher affirmed that people prefer the good things—joy and laughter—over the bad. All else being equal, we would rather sing than mourn, keep than lose, and love than hate. He declared that we ought to enjoy the few days we have under the sun. He did *not* say that life being what it is, we ought to just play our days away. To move in this direction would violate everything he taught in 2:1–11. Still, it is important that we grasp this message as well—that life is short and it ought not to be spent in self-deprivation and misery.

It is noteworthy that the call to enjoy life is connected to an exhortation to fear God (3:12–15). We are mortals, governed by time, so everything we do is fleeting. But our mortality also implies that we ought to enjoy our days under the sun, and that we must fear God. God can give us peace and happiness, and He can afflict us in our mortal weakness. But if we revere Him, accept the fact that we are mortal and no longer fight against the times and seasons that God has ordained for us, then we can rejoice heartily as we journey through our seasons of life.

- *We are creatures of time and governed by*
- *time. We will never find peace as long as we*
- *deny this and refuse to accept the reality that*
- *every aspect of the journey of life has its*
- *place. We must acknowledge that our work*
- *is of this world and will pass away as surely*
- *as we will ourselves. But if we can accept our*
- *mortality and revere God, we can also*
- *appreciate the beauty of the seasons of life*
- *and even enjoy ourselves along the way.*

ON POLITICS (3:15c–17)

"God seeks the persecuted" is another "proleptic conclusion" of the sort we have seen the Teacher use before. As he prepared to enter the area of

"But God seeks the pursued."

The Hebrew of the last line of verse 15 literally says, "But God seeks the pursued." Almost all translations take it to mean something like, "God will call the past to account." However, the word *seek* in Hebrew never means to "call to account" and the word *pursued* never means "the past." In fact, the expression "the pursued" always means "persecuted people" and the verb "seek" in a context like this means to "bring justice in behalf of an innocent victim." Thus, the line means "God seeks [justice] for the persecuted." This line goes with verses 16 and 17 rather than with the preceding section. This is not a discussion of time; it is the Teacher's first look at politics and injustice.

political corruption and oppression, he began by telling us what his conclusion will be: Only God will set right all the evil which people have done to one another.

Certainly, as he looked around, the world did not look like a place where justice prevailed. To the contrary, in the "place of justice" (that is, in the law courts, the bureaucracy, the nobility, the royal court) injustice was everywhere. The very people to whom the oppressed turn for relief were in league with their oppressors. In ancient Israel as in every other place and time, judges and officials took bribes for rendering verdicts favorable to the rich and powerful. In verse 17, therefore, the Teacher affirmed what he had already declared in verse 15c: God is the judge of all the earth, and He will bring vengeance upon the corrupt.

■ *The Teacher's opening comments on political*
■ *power focused on the cruel fact of depravity*
■ *and oppression at all levels of government.*
■ *The very purpose of government—the curbing*
■ *of vice and the protection of the weak—had*
■ *been co-opted, and it acted in behalf of the*
■ *evil. Nevertheless, the Teacher also began his*
■ *analysis of government with assurance that*
■ *God sees all and judges all.*

ON DEATH (3:18–22)

This is, for Christian readers, perhaps the most unnerving section of all of Ecclesiastes. The Teacher appeared to deny (or at least seriously question) the whole idea of afterlife. He said that we are like the animals, have the same fate that they have (in that both people and animals die), and that we have no advantage over the animals. Thus, all is "meaningless" (*heel*), and the best we can do is to "enjoy" our works. He seemed to say that death is the end for us so we might as well enjoy life while we can.

The NKJV and a few other versions soften the blow somewhat by translating verse 21 as, "Who knows the spirit of the sons of men, which goes upward, and the spirit of the animal, which goes down to the earth?" This rendition, however, is certainly wrong. The Hebrew means, "Who knows whether the spirit of man goes upward and the spirit of the animal goes downward to the earth?" Even without this verse, the Teacher's attitude toward common notions of afterlife was highly skeptical. It is clear that he had little use for popular notions of eternal life that apparently were popular in his day (and are popular in our own as well).

This passage, however, does not contradict the rest of the Bible, and it certainly is not at odds with the New Testament. The foundation for eternal life in the Bible is always the resurrection. In Ezekiel 37:1–14, Israel the people of God were restored not by coming back as spirits but by a resurrection from the grave. Dry bones came together, flesh came upon them, and the Spirit of God made them live again. Job declared, "After my skin is destroyed . . . in my flesh I shall see God" (Job 19:26 NKJV).

The New Testament affirms that the victory over death and our hope of eternal life is in the resurrection of Jesus. Especially in 1 Cor. 15, it teaches us that our hope of eternal life depends entirely on whether God has raised Jesus from the dead. Without the resurrection, Paul said, we are completely lost (1 Cor. 15:12–19). Like many peoples of the ancient world, many today believe in a kind of unearthly afterlife in which our spirits either continue on in some kind of heaven or are reincarnated. This idea seems similar to the biblical concept of heaven but is in reality far from it because it leaves out what is central to the biblical concept of eternal life—the resurrection of the body. Death lost its power over us when Jesus stood before His disciples and said, "Reach out your hand and put it into my side" (John 20:27).

■ *In this text, the Teacher calls on us to face the*
■ *harsh reality of our mortality. This is the*
■ *very thing that people want to avoid, and it is*
■ *also the reason why they hold to all kinds of*
■ *strange ideas about afterlife or reincarna-*
■ *tion. But if we look reality in the face, we can*
■ *live the way we should. Facing our mortality*
■ *means that we recognize the fleeting nature*
■ *of this world, enjoy our days under the sun,*
■ *and fear God. Although this text does not*
■ *explicitly add this point, it also means that*
■ *we look to God and to the resurrection for*
■ *salvation from the grip of death.*

ON POLITICS (4:1–3)

This text, like a number of passages in Ecclesi-astes, comes across as profoundly and even pathetically cynical. The Teacher was so pessi-mistic about the possibility of finding good gov-ernment that he thought the dead were better off than the living!

It is important to observe, however, that the Teacher regularly used the kind of *hyperbole* that often appears in ancient Near Eastern texts. Hyperbole is when a person exaggerates for effect, and this was a common rhetorical technique in the ancient Near East. Jesus, for example, did not want us to literally pluck out our eyes or literally hate our parents (Matt. 5:29; Luke 14:26).

In the same manner, when the Teacher said that it was better to be dead—and better still never to have lived—than to see the kind of corrup-tion and oppression that went on in the name of government, his words should not be taken too literally. What he asserted in the strongest pos-sible terms is that oppression and official mis-conduct are heinous, offensive, and destructive practices. If anything, his words meant that oppression robs life of joy and thus makes it not worth living. He had already claimed that God had made everything beautiful in its time and that if one can go through the seasons of life with contentment, accepting one's own mortal-ity, then life can be joyful. This is impossible, however, if a person is controlled by external powers which show contempt for the weak and have no regard for what is right.

■ *The Teacher mourned for people who suffer*
■ *oppression because they have no "comforter"*
■ *and thus have no opportunity to enjoy life. It*
■ *is in this sense that life under oppression is*
■ *not worth living.*

ON WEALTH (4:4–8)

Once again, the Teacher returned to the topic of wealth. This text is in three parts:

1. An observation on the motive for seeking wealth (v. 4);
2. Two proverbs on laziness and labor (vv. 5–6); and
3. A look at the "workaholic" (vv. 7–8).

He began by declaring that the quest for wealth is driven by a desire to have more than one's neighbor. People cannot stand the idea of others having something they do not have. In American idiom, we speak of "keeping up with the Joneses." Once again, the Teacher's words should not be pressed too literally. All greed does not grow out of competition with neighbors. Some people are greedy because they are very insecure about the future, for example. But certainly many people are greedy out of pure desire to outdo other people in the race to acquire things. This is truly a race for the unattainable. There will always be people who have more than us, and *having* more than someone else will never give satisfaction.

In verses 5–6 the Teacher set two apparently opposing proverbs alongside one another. The

The two proverbs of verses 5–6 strike a balance: Work, but do not work too much; enjoy life, but do not be lazy.

Verses 7–8 paint a portrait of a "workaholic." This person works for the sake of work and acquires for the sake of acquisition. It is not a matter of providing for family or even for a cause. Although the figure in verse 8 seems to be a bachelor, we can easily imagine a person who does have a spouse and family and yet neglects them for the sake of gaining money. Any pretense such a person has about doing it all for the sake of family is hollow.

first says that laziness is self-destructive folly. A fool folds his hands and consumes his own flesh. That is, such a person does not produce anything and eventually starves. In short, sloth is a self-destructive vice, and a person must work in order to have a good life.

The second proverb, however, tells us that a single handful with peace is better than two handfuls with toil and vexation. The message is that we should not spend so much time working that we can never enjoy the things we possess. A single handful represents having just enough money to get by, over against the abundance that two handfuls symbolize. A person should not spend his entire life in work; eventually we should recognize that enough is enough, cut down on the number of hours spent working, and enjoy life.

■ *The Teacher wants us to avoid the poverty of*
■ *indolence and the emptiness of living for*
■ *wealth and possessions—a life that is "chas-*
■ *ing after wind."*

QUESTIONS TO GUIDE YOUR STUDY

1. Why is the search for wisdom and knowledge often frustrating and at times absurd?
2. What is the Teacher's assessment of wealth as the greatest good in life?
3. What does the Teacher observe about the times and seasons of life?

ON FRIENDSHIP (4:9–12)

This simple passage lists four benefits of friendship. First, cooperation among friends makes for more efficient labor (v. 9). Two friends working together could build houses for each of them much easier than the two could do by working individually on their own houses.

Second, friends can assist one another when trouble strikes (v. 10). "Falling" in this text represents any kind of trouble that may befall a person. Trouble may take the form of illness or an injury, emotional trauma (such as the death of a loved one), loss of employment, or any other of the countless ordeals that overwhelm people.

Third, friends give emotional comfort to one another (v. 11). In this verse, lying down together has nothing to do with sexual activity. It alludes to the fact that desert nights were often very cold, and travelers had nothing but each other to keep them warm (firewood being very scarce). Metaphorically, the body warmth which friends give to each other represents the solace and encouragement one gets from a friend, particularly from a friend who shares the same hardships. This is one reason that wartime friendships are so close; people have gone through harrowing experiences together.

Fourth, friends can protect one another from enemies (v. 12). This continues to be true today, even in contexts where physical violence is not involved. Friends can protect each other in the work environment from an unscrupulous employee who gets ahead by slandering colleagues.

It is significant that friendship is one aspect of life that the Teacher does not declare to be vanity (*heel*). In a world where so much time is spent in the foolish pursuit of wealth, fame, power, and knowledge—where so much energy is wasted chasing wind—efforts spent at maintaining strong friendship are wisely expended.

■ *True friendship is a precious possession in this*
■ *mortal life. People who find true soul mates are*
■ *richer than persons with money only and wiser*
■ *than those with learning only.*

ON POLITICS (4:13–16)

This text is an "example story," a narrative that tells a short story with a moral lesson. Another example of an example story in wisdom literature is Prov. 7:6–27. In this story, we learn how quickly power passes out of a person's hands.

The interpretation of this story is complicated by the fact that the translation is uncertain. There are grounds for translating the text as follows:

A poor but wise youth is better than an old but foolish king who no longer knows how to take a warning, even though he (the old king) arose from prison to become king, in spite of having been born poor in his kingdom. I saw that all the living, those who walked about under the sun, were with the latter youth who would arise after him. There is no end to all the people, to all who were prior to them, and those who came later were not pleased with him (the latter youth). This too is meaningless, a chasing after wind.

The Teacher had in mind two people who rose to power from obscure roots. The first had been born into poverty and he rose to become king, although he had spent time in prison. He was quick to appraise a situation, decisive, and flexible in responding to challenges. But as he became old, he lost his ability to react quickly and came to rely on the exercise of power alone. In short, he became foolish.

In time there arose a second youth who was very much like the king in his younger days. Using his brains and charisma rather than brute force, he supplanted the aged king. The people who had cheered the old king when he rose to power were pleased to throw their support behind the upstart. Yet neither of these kings achieved lasting power or praise. In time, the new king would fall just like his predecessor.

- *In the quest for power, one person succeeds*
- *another, and in time that person is sup-*
- *planted by another still. Past success is no*
- *guarantee of future achievements. Power is*
- *by nature fleeting, and the crowd is fickle.*

ON RELIGION (5:1–7)

This text is in two parallel parts, as follows:

A: Admonition: Worship in humble silence, not with grand sacrifices (v. 1).

  B: Warning: Do not speak quickly before God (v. 2).

  C: Proverb: Big dreams are the mark of fools (v. 3).

A: Admonition: If you make a vow, fulfill it (v. 4).

  B: Warning: Make no vow you cannot keep (vv. 5–6).

  C: Proverb: Big dreams are the mark of fools (v. 7a).

Conclusion: Fear God (v. 7b).

Verse 1 could be translated like this: "Proceed with reverence when you go to the house of God. It is more acceptable to listen than when fools give sacrifice. Those who merely listen do not have the opportunity to do wrong."

People who approach God with many words, even with many vows, show that they lack reverence for God, and they fail to grasp the nature of God. His grandeur, represented by the fact that He is "in heaven," is such that efforts to

The phrase translated "proceed with reverence" is literally "guard your steps," and the phrase translated "do not have the opportunity" is literally "do not know how." The point is that the best way to approach God's house is in silent reverence. If you come with long prayers, promises, and boasts of great gifts you intend to bring, you are likely to get into real trouble. The parallel admonition in verse 4 tells us to fulfill whatever vows we make.

impress Him are truly ridiculous. Indeed, the line "he is in heaven and you are on earth" is one of the great texts of Ecclesiastes. It is a powerful description of what it means to be mortal. The practical outcome of this lesson is that if you make a vow, you should fulfill it as quickly as possible. God is not amused by flippant vows that are ill-considered when made and then are forgotten or neglected.

People who make such vows also have to face the embarrassment of having to declare their vow a "mistake" before the "messenger." The identity of the "messenger" is debated, but it may be (1) God Himself, (2) an avenging angel, or (3) a prophet, priest, or messenger from the Temple. It is probably the latter, a temple messenger sent to collect from a person who has not fulfilled his pledge.

The proverbs in verse 3 and verse 7a state that people who make big promises are "dreamers" or "big-talkers" who try to cover their inadequacies with boasts of great gifts and deeds to come. Big words are not the mark of a big person; they are the mark of a fool.

The sum of this text (v. 7b) is that a person should fear God. It is important to see how Ecclesiastes conveys a message of grace. Because we are mortal, weak, and of the earth, we have no hope of impressing God—certainly not with hollow vows that we cannot keep. For this reason, the Teacher stops just short of recommending that we not make vows at all (v. 5). But this is not a reason for despair in our relationship to God. It only means that we can give up on trying to gain His favor with impressive deeds. Recognizing our mortality, we can do nothing but fall upon the mercy of God. Since He is in heaven and we are on earth, we must have His grace to survive.

■ *Reverence for God and silent worship are*
■ *better than showy acts meant to impress Him*
■ *and others. Worse yet is the making of hol-*
■ *low promises. Our goal in worship is not to*
■ *impress God but to submit to Him.*

ON POLITICS (5:8–9)

Returning to the issue of corruption in politics, the Teacher advised us not to be surprised when we find it. Because there are many layers of bureaucracy in government with many officials in all those layers: "One official is eyed by a higher one, and over them both are others higher still." In other words, there are so many individuals involved at so many levels that perversion of justice is bound to occur at some point. The very administrative system that is supposed to check corruption contributes to it! The Teacher is not being cynical or indifferent to the suffering of the poor. He has already stated in the strongest possible terms that he considered this to be so evil that it made life hardly worth living (4:1–3). At this point, however, he counseled realism and acceptance of the fact that there is much evil in this world. His words in 4:1–3 might be taken to mean that he was driven to despair; this text restores balance: A person should run neither to cynicism nor despair.

English versions of the Bible translate 5:9 in a number of ways, most of which do not fit the context. Probably the best rendition is: "But all in all, an advantage for the land is this: a king, for the sake of agriculture." The point is that whether we like it or not, government is necessary. The example cited is agriculture. In the ancient world, the royal governments had to maintain aqueducts and other common water sources, protect the fields against enemies and bandits, ensure property rights, and do other related things to keep the agricultural economy running.

Even if there is corruption in government, anarchy and rebellion are not the answer. The Teacher calls us to a balanced, mature view of life.

■ *We should not be shocked by the fact that*
■ *some members of a government bureaucracy*
■ *are evil. Furthermore, we need to recognize*
■ *that no matter how evil it may be, govern-*
■ *ment is necessary.*

QUESTIONS TO GUIDE YOUR STUDY
1. What are four benefits of friendship?
2. What is the Teacher's counsel regarding religion?
3. What does the Teacher say regarding corruption in politics?

ON WEALTH (5:10–6:6)

The Teacher now moves into another lengthy discourse on wealth. It is probably significant that he devotes such long texts to this subject (see also 2:1–11). This passage divides into two parts. First, in 5:10–15, he listed reasons for not making the acquisition of wealth the object of one's life. Second, in 5:16–6:6, he reflected on what it means to enjoy one's days under the sun and on whether having money contributes to happiness.

In 5:10–15, he gave seven reasons why a person should not pursue riches:

First, wealth is addictive and gives no satisfaction (v. 10). "He who loves abundance" never gets enough of it and is never happy with what he has.

Second, wealth attracts human parasites (v. 11a). Wealthy people are surrounded by those who think the rich are morally obligated to support them.

Third, excess wealth does the owner no good. He already has more than enough to meet all his needs, and thus he cannot do anything with his extra money but stare at it (v. 11b).

Fourth, excess money does not give a person peace and security but only adds to his worries. He frets late at night on his bed about whether his investments are safe from misfortune and crime (v. 12).

Fifth, love of money causes a person to hoard what he ought to spend for his own benefit (v. 13). Such a person should spend or give away a sum of money, but he is unable to part with his wealth. He will never experience the happiness he could get from spending money on himself or another person, or by giving money away.

Sixth, wealth is by nature insecure; it can vanish quickly and leave a person without the means to care for his family (v. 14). Want is all the harder to bear for a person who once had money.

Seventh, a person definitely loses all his wealth at death. It is the ultimate example of *heel* (vanity).

The miser cannot experience joy. To the contrary, he spends his time in gloom and sorrow (5:16–17). The "darkness" in which he eats represents misery and isolation, and it anticipates the gloom of Sheol, his final destination.

To be able to enjoy life, however, is a gift from God (5:18–20). No person, no matter how rich he or she may be, can enjoy life without God's grace. It is remarkable that the person who has joy from God rarely reflects upon the brevity of his life (5:20). Elsewhere, the Teacher will make a point of claiming that we should take time to reflect upon death and the brevity of life (7:4). It is probably correct to say that we should have a healthy awareness of our mortality, but we should avoid an unhealthy fixation on death. The Teacher demanded that we face the fact of our mortality, but he also declared that a joyful life is not dominated by thoughts of death. Those who love God are too busy enjoying themselves to take time to be morose.

"So teach us to number our days, that we may present to Thee a heart of wisdom" (Ps. 90:12, NASB).

In 6:1–6, the Teacher described a hypothetical person who is superrich by the standards of the ancient world. He had money, things, honor among people, and a hundred children. More than that, he lived 2,000 years (v. 6)! For the ancient Israelite, wealth, children, and long life were the standards for judging whether a person was rich. The Teacher contrasted this man with a fetus who is stillborn. Thus, the ultimate "have" (the superrich person) is contrasted with the ultimate "have-not" (a stillborn fetus, who never saw the sun, never had a name, and never had any experiences).

In most translations, 6:3 seems to say that the rich person did not receive a proper burial, and the Teacher appears to be saying that his life was worthless if he didn't receive a proper funeral. This makes little sense. Most wealthy people receive elaborate funerals, but it is hard to see how the Teacher would think that a funeral would make their lives worthwhile. Instead, the translation should reflect the fact that it was the stillborn child, not the rich man, who got no funeral. It should read, "Even if he does not receive a proper burial, the stillborn child, I assert, is better off than the rich man." The point the teacher is making is that no person should envy the unhappy rich. As far as the Teacher was concerned, a fetus that died before seeing the light of day was better off than the rich person.

The Teacher was not trying to teach us anything about the eternal destiny of stillborn children in this passage. In saying that the fetus "departs in darkness," he meant that it never had a place under the sun.

■ *The pursuit of wealth is folly. It will not*
■ *bring happiness. Those who are unhappy but*
■ *rich are not in an enviable position.*

TRANSITION (6:7–9)

What is the topic of this text? It begins by speaking of how people work to meet their physical needs. This implies that the topic is still the pursuit of wealth (v. 7). In verse 8, however, the focus is on how the intellectual has no real advantage over a fool. This seems to imply that the topic has shifted back to wisdom. Finally, verse 9 speaks of the quest for more and more, the roving appetite.

"A worker's appetite works for him, for his hunger urges him on" Prov. 16:26, NASB.

This passage is transitional in that it moves us from the discussion of the pursuit of wealth (5:10–6:6) to a discussion of the pursuit of wisdom and knowledge (6:10–7:4).

■ *The intellectual seeks knowledge with the*
■ *same zeal by which the miser seeks money.*
■ *Both are driven by their "appetites." Their*
■ *motives, moreover, are not really all that dif-*
■ *ferent. Both seek permanence and signifi-*
■ *cance in the face of death and a tumble into*
■ *meaninglessness.*

ON WISDOM AND DEATH (6:1–7:4)

This text appears exceedingly pessimistic. The Teacher seems to say that learning is a waste of time, that death stares every person in the face, and that sorrow is the only appropriate response to the realities of life. It is not quite so bleak, however. The text is divided into two parts:

The Hebrew word *adam* ("man") appears four times in 6:10–12. As a general word, it refers to the human race, but it is also the name of the first man: Adam. This usage of the word is not accidental; the Teacher points us back to the story of Gen. 2—3. In verse 10, "Whatever exists has already been named" looks back to Adam's naming of all the animals (Gen. 2:19). The Teacher declared that the wisest of men has already come and has done the most profound of intellectual work, the cataloging of the works of creation. Thus, it is futile for one of his descendants to suppose he or she can achieve immortality by repeating what Adam has already done. Intellectual achievement will not allow us to become like God. It was through their search for the "knowledge of good and evil" that humans attempted to become godlike.

reflections of the meaning of humanity's fall into sin (6:10–12) and teachings on why it is necessary to confront one's mortality (7:1–4).

The word translated "man" is *adam*, the same word that appears in Genesis as Adam. The Teacher looks back to the story of the Fall to understand our human predicament.

The second part of verse 10 should be translated, "And it is known that he is *adam* and that he cannot dispute with one stronger than he." The word *known* implies that what Adam really discovered was not knowledge that made him godlike but the knowledge of how much weaker he was than God. His quest for knowledge ended in disaster; the tree of the knowledge of good and evil was the door to death. What he discovered was that he was truly *adam*. The Hebrew word *adam* is related to the word *adamah*, "soil." It implies that man is physical, weak, made of dirt, and destined to decay.

Now that we have fallen, and now that the knowledge of good and evil has enslaved us in death, we realize that an excess of words (knowledge) will not save us (v. 11). In fact, our limitations are great. We cannot know the future, and such limited knowledge cannot save us from our human predicament (v. 12).

In 7:1–4, the Teacher gave us a series of proverbs to let us know that the wisest thing we can do is take the lesson of our mortality to heart. In 7:1, he began with what is a very conventional proverb, that a good name is better than fine perfume, but then he jolted us with an unexpected second line: The day of death is better than the day of birth. In both cases, what seems to be better (expensive luxuries, and the day of birth) proves not to be so.

The reason for this surprising conclusion—that a death is better than a birth—is that a death forces us to take stock of reality. The reality is that we are all headed to the same place, that life is very short, and that all our works are doomed to perish with us. If we take this lesson to heart, we will spend our time on earth wisely and will not waste our lives in vexation or frivolity.

The point is not that we should be miserable but that we should face facts soberly and make good decisions about how to spend our limited time. This is the reason why people who have had a brush with death can claim that it was the best thing that ever happened to them.

- Knowledge alone will not save us or allow us
- to escape the fact of our mortality. In fact, the
- wisest thing we can do is face death and
- reckon with the issue of how we ought to
- spend our days.

TRANSITION (7:5–6)

These verses consist of more proverbs on the importance of facing life soberly. Like 7:1, 7:5 is a proverb which states that the thing that seems more painful—a wise man's rebuke—is actually better than what seems fun—listening to silly songs. These two verses continue the theme begun in 6:10–7:4. The laughter of fools is probably their laughing at wisdom and the careful, cautious words of the sages. They consider traditional wisdom to be so much rubbish. This naturally leads into the next section, a text that deals with cynicism in politics.

ON WISDOM AND POLITICS (7:7–9)

How does "oppression" or "extortion" make a wise man a fool? Oppression or extortion may not affect him directly or cause him to lose his senses. Rather, these make a fool out of him in the eyes of the world in that his advice is seen to be wrong. The sage teaches his pupils to always be just and to live with integrity. But the pupils

Throughout that ancient Near East, wisdom teachers taught that it was the duty of officials to protect the defenseless and to see that justice was carried out. This advice, then as now, was often ignored.

look around and see some very unscrupulous people getting very rich. Political cynics could look at the situation, see that only the ruthless get ahead and that their power is unchecked, and laugh the wise to scorn. In their eyes, the sages have been made into fools by the facts of political life.

Put another way, the cruel facts of the "real" world make the ideals of the wise look stupid. Similarly, cynics would see that the way to get ahead and get along is through bribery and corruption. Thus, the fact of the political world would seem to undermine any attempts to maintain integrity.

In 7:8–9, however, the Teacher counseled patience. In the end, the way of wisdom is shown to be right. Thus, it is not wise to become provoked, agitated, or despondent over the apparent facts of political life. To hold on to anger over the political situation is just another form of folly. It is best to let God and time do their work, awaiting the justice that will finally come.

■ *Cynics and fools laugh at the "stupidity" of*
■ *trying to maintain righteousness in a world*
■ *where corruption is the norm and where*
■ *money rules everything. But a person should*
■ *patiently wait to see how things turn out.*
■ *Wisdom is justified in the long run.*

TRANSITION (7:10)

This is yet another transitional text. It looks back to the previous text in the sense that people often observe the crime, corruption, and abuse going on all around them and yearn for the "good old days" when people did not behave this way. But every generation has its own corruption and sin. It is not wise to suppose that there was once a time when everything was good and there was no corruption. On the other hand, this text also looks ahead to the next section, a discussion of money and economic good times and bad times. Again, in times of economic hardship, people tend to get nostalgic for earlier days.

ON WISDOM AND WEALTH (7:11–14)

In this passage the Teacher brings together his discussions of both wisdom and money, calling upon us to have a balanced, realistic understanding of the issues. He has criticized the quest for wisdom and the desire for riches. On the other hand, both wisdom and money have value. Both are "shelters," meaning that both afford protection from the storms of life. On the whole, however, wisdom is superior. Its "advantage" is that it can allow a person to avoid dangers and thus lead to the preservation of his life.

The Teacher asked a rhetorical question in verse 13, "Who can straighten what he [God] has made crooked?" This looks back to the proverb found in Eccl. 1:15, "What is twisted cannot be straightened." The point is that there are situations that we cannot understand and problems we cannot solve. In hard times as in good, we should accept everything as from the hand of God and be content with His reign. We cannot foretell the future, but we can accept the fact that God controls it.

Wisdom teachers in the ancient Near East sometimes cast their teachings in the form of riddles or enigmas. The Teacher used enigmatic proverbs in this passage to make his point.

■ *Although neither wealth nor wisdom can*
■ *save us from the limitations of our mortality,*
■ *both have their place in life. We should*
■ *accept our limitations, fear God, and live*
■ *balanced lives.*

ON VIRTUE AND SIN (7:15–29)

At first glance, this text is a hodgepodge of ideas that seems to have no center. On closer inspection, however, we discover that at the heart of the whole passage is the question of virtue and evil in people. The passage is in three parts:

1. A warning against religious excess (vv. 15–18);
2. Coping with evil in others (vv. 19–22); and
3. The search for a man or woman of virtue (vv. 23–29).

At the opening, the Teacher declared that during his days of *heel* (that is, the fleeting days of his life) he had seen all kinds of monstrosities, including the righteous person whose life is cut short and the wicked person who thrives. At first glance, the Teacher's conclusion seems outrageous: "Do not be overrighteous, neither be overwise—why destroy yourself?" Is he saying that a person should sin a little in order to maintain a balanced life? One might well draw this conclusion from the following line, "Do not be overwicked."

It is important, however, to take note of what "righteous" and "wise" mean in this context. In this text, "righteousness" refers to following the teachings that we should live restrained, controlled lives, and "wisdom" refers to the teach-

If "righteousness" or "religion" is defined as love for God and obedient submission to Him, then it is hard to know how a person can be "overly righteous." On the other hand, if we take these terms to refer to a life of strict "scruples," then it is possible for a person to go too far. In short, if a person is so burdened with rules, scruples, and obligations that life becomes a burden and all joy is swallowed up in duty, then indeed he or she is overly "righteous" and overly "wise."

ings of the "wise," the movement that tried to gain mastery of life through intellectual understanding of the ways of the world. Another way of expressing it is to say that "righteousness and wisdom" here stand for what we may describe as a "religious life." It all comes down to how we define "religious" and "righteous" in this context.

The last line of verse 18 should be translated, "He who fears God comes out with all of them." What are "all" the things that such a person comes away with? What are the different things a person should "grasp" and not "let go of." Surely the Teacher does not mean that we can hold on to righteousness and wickedness at the same time. Many people have destroyed themselves trying to do that. Rather, "all" refers to all the topics in the book of Ecclesiastes.

Finally, we must take note of how important the "fear of God" is in this part of the discussion. What matters is not how wise, scrupulous, or disciplined we are. What really matters is whether we fear God. In this sense, Ecclesiastes points us to grace.

Verse 19 is a proverb that at first seems to have nothing to do with this discussion. It has meaning, however, when read in light of the following verse. Because there is so much evil in society—indeed because no one is wholly pure—a city needs wisdom (one wise person) to help control evil and maintain order more than it needs brute force (ten rulers). A wise person knows that there is evil in the people all around, but he manages to lead, inspire, and keep order anyway. A bad leader simply gives orders and demands that they be obeyed.

We can hold to wisdom without seeking our salvation in wisdom. We can make use of money without entering the foolish quest for riches and pleasures. We can do what is right, fear God, and also enjoy life, eating and drinking with friends in the few days under the sun which we are allotted.

Verse 21 is another proverb that is explained by the verse that follows. The point is that all of us know that we have said things about others that were rude, hurtful, or cruel. We also should realize that we should be forbearing when others say the same about us.

Verses 23–29 seem particularly harsh in what they say about women. The best place to begin to understand this passage is the last verse, where the Teacher says that God made humanity upright but they have gone after many schemes. This alludes to the story of Creation and the Fall, where God made man and woman "very good" but they turned against him and fell into sin. They sought "many schemes" and went in their own way. This text, then, is basically a reflection on the meaning of humankind's fall into sin.

The really difficult text is verses 26–28, where the Teacher declared that the man who pleases God escapes the woman whose heart is a "net" and whose hands are "chains." He also asserts that he has found only "one man in a thousand" but not a single woman. Some people interpret this passage to mean that the "woman" is the prostitute or even a personification of folly, but nothing in the passage supports this.

The solution is that the Teacher is reflecting on the story of the Fall. In that passage, the woman received word that because she now was without God, her family life would be painful and even deadly (Gen. 3:15). Childbirth would be filled with agony. More than that, God said, "Your desire will be for your husband, and he will rule over you." In this context, "desire" is not sexual or loving, and "rule" is not kind or benevolent. This is a text that tells how sin will

Verses 19–22 tell us that we need to learn how to get along with people, lead people, and get the best from people, even though they are all sinners. Another way of saying this is that we need to understand what *agape* love is all about.

The key to interpreting 7:26–29 is to recognize that it builds upon Gen. 3:15—a text that teaches that because of sin, family life will be filled with grief.

ruin domestic life, not a text that portrays God's will for domestic life.

Furthermore, this line has an exact parallel in Gen. 4:7, where God told Cain concerning sin, "It desires to have you, but you must master it." In that text, clearly, "desire" was not loving and "rule" was without compassion. In short, Gen. 3:15 said that because sin had come into the world, the relationship that ought to be the most loving would be the most ferocious battleground. Women would "desire" to control their husbands, but the men, by virtue of physical size and economic power, would "rule" their wives. It would be a miserable situation for everyone.

The Teacher is therefore speaking, from a man's point of view, of the conflict that tears apart relationships between men and women. Speaking as a man, he declared that many women are traps and snares to their husbands. Thus, he said that he has (very rarely) found a man with whom he could have a noncompetitive friendship that was free of scheming and the desire to control. Many people find that they can have one or perhaps two friendships that are without conflict.

Just as God told Eve that sin would destroy her primary arena, the home, in Gen. 3:17–19 he declared that the man's primary arena activity, the field, would also fight against him.

The Teacher's point is not that marriage is a bad thing or that righteous people should avoid it. Rather, those who fear God can have a marriage that is characterized by love instead of strife. But just as sin has corrupted the political realm, so it has also corrupted marriage.

■ *The Teacher here took a serious look at*
■ *human virtue and sin. He concluded that we*
■ *should fear God but not be driven by reli-*
■ *gious scruples, that we should be forbearing*
■ *in the face of the fact that all people are sin-*
■ *ners, and that it is only through the fear of*
■ *God that we can have a happy domestic life.*

TRANSITION (8:1)

This verse is another transitional text. It looks back to the quest to understand situations and in particular to the wise man's ability to govern unruly sinners (7:19–20). This text also looks forward to how a wise administrator can earn the king's favor (8:2–6).

"His face shines"

The expression "his face shines" means that a superior is showing favor to a subordinate, as in the expression, "May the LORD make his face shine upon you" (Num. 6:25). Thus, this passage looks ahead to 8:2–6, which describes how a wise subordinate can stay in the king's good graces.

This verse is perhaps best translated, "Who is like the wise man, and who can explain a situation? A person's wisdom makes his face shine and changes a grim expression." One might naturally assume that wisdom makes the wise person's face shine, but this is probably not the meaning.

ON POLITICS (8:2–6)

This text counsels wise subordination and tact toward a ruler. A person is bound to obey a superior because it is a duty to do so before God. In addition, tactless and incessant opposition to a leader never works well. It is better to look for the "proper time" to stand up for a cause. This is sometimes hard to do, for when one is convinced that people in leadership positions are following a foolish path, "misery weighs heavily" upon the perceptive subordinate. Here, too, there is a time to speak and a time to be silent.

TRANSITION (8:7–8)

In yet another transitional text, the Teacher first spoke of our inability to tell what the future holds (v. 7). This looks back to the previous text, which referred to a counselor before his king. It was the duty of the counselor to give sound advice, and the ability to do so depended in large measure on how well the counselor could determine what was likely to happen in the future (thus, in pagan countries, many high counselors were also predictors of the future). However, he then spoke of the great disasters of life, including storms ("wind"), death, and war. He also spoke unexpectedly of how justice eventually catches up with the wicked ("evil will not deliver those who practice it," NASB). This leads into the next text (8:9–9:1), a discussion of God's governance of the world. It is also noteworthy that the Teacher has just spoken of dealing with human kings in their administration of justice; now the text speaks of the ultimate King.

QUESTIONS TO GUIDE YOUR STUDY

1. What is the Teacher's counsel regarding the pursuit of wealth?
2. In what sense is death a valuable teacher?
3. What does the Teacher mean in asking, "Who can straighten what God has bent?"
4. In what way has sin corrupted marriage?

ON THEODICY (8:9–9:1)

This text is in three parts:

1. The prosperity of the wicked (vv. 9–11);
2. An affirmation of God's divine justice, (vv. 12–13); and
3. The apparent perversion of justice in the world, and the Teacher's surprising conclusion (8:14–9:1).

Theodicy

Theodicy is the defense of God's goodness in light of two other realities: God's all-powerful nature and the existence of evil.

Verses 9–10 pose some special challenges in the Hebrew language, but a case can be made for the following translation: "All this I have seen, and I have given attention to every deed done under the sun while man rules men to their hurt. And in such circumstances I saw the wicked buried. And people came and attended the funeral, and the wicked were praised in the city where they had behaved in so wicked a manner." Contrary to some translations, a person does not rule over others to his own hurt; if

49

that were the case, the Teacher would not be concerned about injustice and oppression. The Hebrew speaks of going to the "holy place." This is not the Temple or a shrine; it is a euphemism for a burial plot or funeral. Unclean bodies rendered a person unclean.

As the Teacher looked over the world, he saw the oppression of the weak by the strong, a topic that he had already discussed. He observed a funeral where a powerful man whom everyone knew to have been corrupt and cruel was buried, but then he was praised extravagantly. This, coupled with the fact that criminals of all kinds frequently get away unpunished, leaves people cynical and inclined to want to do evil themselves.

In verses 12–13, however, the Teacher asserted his faith in the justice of God. There may be injustice and absurdity in abundance for now, but he was sure that in his own time and way God would deal with evil and evil people. It is striking that he did not rationalize or defend his belief. It was a statement of faith.

In verse 14, however, the Teacher brought up an even more profound challenge to God's goodness. Not only do we see examples of evil people getting away with their crimes; we also see reverse justice in operation. The good people sometimes get what ought to go to a wicked person, and the evil people sometimes seem to be rewarded with health, wealth, and happiness. The world not only has evil in it, but it also seems absolutely wicked.

The Teacher resolved this problem in a way that is perhaps very surprising to us. First, he declared that people should enjoy life and not deprive themselves of happiness by being upset over the problem of evil (v. 15). This is not the kind of answer we expect! It seems to be a mindless flight from the problem. In fact, however, it is very much in keeping with the Teacher's recommendations throughout the book. Life is full of painful and insoluble problems. If a person could have no peace until every vexation was resolved, then one would never have peace! It is a gift of God to rejoice in this life of *heel*.

Second, the Teacher said that God has deliberately made life unpredictable in order to frustrate those who try to control life (vv. 16–17). Wise people, like the three friends of Job, claim to understand life precisely because they want to be able to manage it. They think that by following certain rules they can avoid all calamities and congratulate themselves when they see problems befall others. But it is precisely here that the Teacher uncovers a profound truth about wisdom. For all its value, wisdom can never be used to control God.

Third, the Teacher concluded that God is sovereign (9:1). Will it be "love" or "hate"? That is, will God show grace to a person, or will He turn against him? In the final analysis, it is God's decision and not ours. This is not to say that the Teacher rejects the idea that God is merciful to the repentant. That is not the issue here. Rather, the point is that a key element in the fear of God is simple acknowledgment that He is in control. Indeed, this returns us to the idea of grace in a fashion that is perhaps uncomfortable for us. We must acknowledge that we really cannot demand anything. We must simply ask Him to be generous. Strangely and yet profoundly, the Teacher declared that evil in the world should lead us to a deeper fear of God.

When wisdom fails, we must simply trust God and realize that we are in His hands. It is more important that we yield to Him than that we know how to master life itself.

■ *Qoheleth resolved the problem of evil in a*
■ *way that some of us may find astonishing.*
■ *Evil in the world leads us to a deeper fear of*
■ *God because we know by life's very uncer-*
■ *tainty that we cannot control God. Those*
■ *who do not fear God, however, see evil in the*
■ *world and are encouraged to do more evil*
■ *themselves.*

TRANSITION (9:2)

This text is transitional in that, like the conclusion of the previous passage, it describes our inability to control life and protect ourselves from its harsher realities by being "wise" or religious. But it also speaks of the "common destiny" of everyone—of death—and thus looks ahead to the next passage.

ON DEATH AND CONTENTMENT (9:3–10)

This text includes further reflections on death (vv. 3–6) and an exhortation to the reader (vv. 7–10). It anticipates his final reflections on death and contentment in 11:7–12:7.

Using the proverb that "a live dog is better off than a dead lion," the Teacher asserted that unlike the dead the living have "hope." His explanation, however, is startling: "For the living know that they will die." It seems their hope is the knowledge that they will die! The actual content of their hope, however, is clarified in the verses that follow. The living have a chance to attain happiness under the sun. This chance has already passed by the dead. The Teacher is saying, "If you are still alive, you still have hope

The Teacher was astounded at the "madness" of humans. They are all living under a sentence of death, and yet they all are consumed by passions. They are filled with love, hatred, jealousy, and envy. In light of the whole book, we could rightly add that people consume their lives with anxiety, work so frantically that they have no hope of attaining happiness, fight for position, power, money, achievement, and victory. At the end of it all, they die, and everything they struggled for vanishes.

of having a good life. Do not despair; find your happiness while you can!"

He developed this idea in verses 7–10. It is liberating to read that God "approves" of what we do in eating, drinking, and enjoying life. It is difficult for religious people to shake the notion that eating is a biological function that we are permitted to practice in order to keep the body alive (much as sex is something we are permitted to practice for the sake of keeping our species alive), but that God certainly does not want us to *enjoy* it. It is hard for us to accept the simple fact that God wants us to enjoy life. But a healthy mind and a true appreciation for grace come only when we embrace the good things God has for us. (This does not justify gluttony for food or sex.)

Some translations give this text an overly dour flavor by translating the phrase, "all your days of *heel*" as "all your meaningless days" (e.g., NIV). In this context, *heel* means "fleeting," and the line should be rendered: "Spend your life with the woman you love all the days of your fleeting life that God has given you under the sun, all your fleeting days, for that is your share in life and in the labor you do under the sun."

Wearing white clothes and anointing the hair represent enjoying life (v. 8). It is the opposite of the dark sackcloth and sad look of a person who is in mourning or fasting. In some cultures, white clothing symbolized mourning; this was not the case in ancient Israel.

The command to face life's tasks with vigor and enthusiasm is more than just encouraging advice. It looks back to the curse on Adam, in which God told him he would face a life of endless toil (Gen. 3:17–19). Here, the Teacher declared that this does not mean that God wants us to be miserable in work, just as the curse upon the woman does not mean that God wants domestic life to be full of conflict. The person who fears God can have a good marriage and an enjoyable job.

■ *Most people avoid the implications of death*
■ *and lead lives of mindless greed and quiet*
■ *desperation. It need not be this way, how-*
■ *ever. Those who recognize the essence of life*
■ *and who submit to God can enjoy the life that*
■ *God gives. The curses of Genesis 3:16–19*
■ *can be reversed.*

TRANSITION (9:11–12)

Again, the Teacher is using a transitional passage. On the one hand, these two verses look back to the previous discussion of death ("a man does not know his time," v. 12). On the other hand, they refer to the fact that skill is not a guarantee of success in our endeavors. This will be important in the next section, a discussion of the realities of political life—a world in which skill and integrity are not always rewarded.

The claim that victory does not always come to the fastest or strongest or wisest is not cynical and it is not meant to lead us to despair. It is simply a truth, as anyone who follows sports understands. Sometimes the person most deserving does not win. We must recognize and accept this fact if we are to find contentment in life. Otherwise, we are very likely to be consumed with a sense of having been cheated. The fact that the Teacher spoke of "time and chance" does not nullify the fact that elsewhere he has spoken of God ruling over all things and determining the fate of people. The same event, viewed from one perspective, is a matter of chance; viewed from another perspective, it is the will of God.

ON POLITICS (9:13–10:17)

This text is a collection of anecdotes, observations, and proverbs, but all center on a common theme—the vagaries of political life. The Teacher in this passage dealt not so much with oppression, the theme of his earlier political remarks, as with the sheer folly and incompetence of political life. This built upon 8:2–6, where he encouraged the wise counselor to be patient and tactful in dealing with a king. Here, he addressed the problem of ineptitude in the political realm more directly. If it seems odd

The Teacher devoted a great deal of attention to practical advice on getting along in the political realm because his original audience was primarily members of the aristocracy who were engaged in government administration.

that the text would devote so much time and space to this issue, remember that the original audience of Ecclesiastes was probably members of the male aristocracy who surrounded and assisted the royal government. Many of the comments here are easily transferable to the business world.

Verses 13–16 consist of an anecdote about a poor man whose wisdom saved a city in a time of military crisis. Nothing is said about how he saved the city (it could have been by wise diplomacy or by devising a brilliant defense) because that does not really matter. The important point is that after the crisis passed, no one bothered to give the man the thanks he was due or even to pay attention to his opinions. The praise and glory probably went to a king or general who deserved none of it! But life is at times very unfair.

The proverbs in 9:17–10:1 all revolve around the central teaching in 9:18 that one sinner destroys much good. In 9:17–18a, the Teacher made the point that wisdom is better than brute force in political life. Both the shouts of a ruler and the weapons of war represent the application of power to a problem; wisdom is the ability to solve a problem by appropriate, measured action.

There is, however, a hitch. The wise can be thwarted by one "sinner" or one bit of stupidity. The "sinner" may be a bad counselor who persuades the king to do the wrong thing or an incompetent ruler who cannot see good advice when it is right in front of his face. Or it may be that one bit of folly by the wise counselor himself so ruins his reputation that his wisdom is no longer heeded.

In administration, even the best plans sometimes get fouled up by the smallest acts of stupidity!

The first half of 10:1 should probably be rendered, "Dead flies make a bowl of perfumer's ointment disgusting." The common translation "Dead flies make perfume stink" is colorful but probably not the best interpretation. It would take a sensitive nose indeed to smell dead flies in a bowl of ointment. The ointment spoken of here is probably the very expensive oils that went into perfume; even something as valuable as that is disgusting if it's filled with dead flies! In the same way, great wisdom can be ruined by a little folly.

In 10:2–7, the Teacher made a series of comments on the fact that in any bureaucracy there will be a number of incompetent people. First, in 10:2, he observed that the wise incline to the right and the fools incline to the left. This has nothing to do with current terminology in which "right" means conservative and "left" means liberal. Rather, since most people are right-handed and, therefore, skillful with the right hand but inept with the left, the point is that fools are visibly incompetent. Verse 3 reinforces this with a pointed proverb: A fool cannot walk down the street without demonstrating to everyone that he is a fool! Verse 4 seems to be something of an aside, but it is related to context.

In a world where imbeciles and frauds often rise to power, the decent and competent subordinate often finds himself in trouble for no reason. He must be patient and realize that this kind of frustration goes with the territory. He should not be quick to abandon his post.

Still, the political realm can be very unfair. In 10:5–7 the Teacher spoke of slaves riding while princes walk. This should not be read in light of modern democratic and egalitarian concepts, as though this were a victory for equality and fraternity. Rather, "princes" are the incompetent. Sometimes the worst people get the big promotions. "Princes" refers to people who are noble and competent while "slaves" refers to people who are ignoble. Bureaucratic structures can be unfair and even absurd, but we must learn to live with these problems patiently.

In 10:8–11, the Teacher turned some common axioms on their heads to make some pointed observations about the realities of life. Verse 8 is a standard axiom to the effect that evil comes to those who plot evil for others. "Digging a pit" describes preparing a trap for someone and "breaking through a wall" refers to breaking into someone's house in order to steal. In both cases, the activity results in the wicked person himself suffering destruction. This, of course, is a very positive lesson on how the wicked suffer. Verse 9, however, teaches that someone who quarries stones or splits logs can also be hurt in the activity. These are not in any sense immoral actions. Verses 8–9 say that it is true that a person can get hurt while doing evil, but a person can also be hurt while going about his job. Life is not always fair.

Verses 10–11 are similar. Wisdom is a good thing; by it, a person can save much wasted effort. On the other hand, sometimes wisdom is too little and too late. The point of 10:8–11 is not that it makes no difference whether a person is righteous or evil or wise or foolish. Wisdom and virtue are assumed to be right. The message is simply that sometimes no matter how hard we try to do the right thing, everything still goes wrong. Again, this is not cynicism. It is simply a matter of learning to deal with this world of *heel*.

In 10:12–15, the Teacher contrasted the wise counselor with the arrogant imbecile. The wise counselor's words are "gracious" in that they are carefully considered, prudent, and tactfully spoken. Such a person is never too sure of his words because he knows that the future may hold

In his final comments on the subject of administration, the Teacher made the point that there is no substitute for good leadership (10:16–17). The diligent leader who uses his position to serve others is contrasted with the self-indulgent ruler who uses his power to satisfy his greed. Of course, being a good leader involves more than refraining from self-indulgence, but the point is that it is very hard to overcome poor leadership.

surprises (10:14b). The bad counselor is cocky, verbose, and deceptive in his self-assurance. Even so, 10:3 states that the folly of such a counselor is so plain that it should be evident to any who cares to examine the matter carefully.

Verse 15 should be translated: "The effort of fools wearies him who does not know the way to town." In other words, they are so bad at giving advice that they cannot even give simple directions without confusing and exasperating the people they talk to. Again, the message is that if one cares to look carefully, it is self-evident who are the good and who are the bad counselors.

■ *Bureaucracy often has a way of overlooking*
■ *competent people and sound advice in favor*
■ *of ideas that are trendy and people who are*
■ *self-promoting. This can lead to frustration*
■ *and bitterness if a person does not prepare*
■ *beforehand. We should not let such frustra-*
■ *tion ruin our joy under the sun.*

TRANSITION (10:18–20)

This is another transitional verse in that it applies to both the previous text on politics and the following text on wealth. The text is made up of three proverbs. The first, verse 18, states that a person must be diligent to maintain a household. This obviously holds true for a single household as well as the whole state. Second, verse 19 asserts that we do need some money to enjoy life; this looks ahead to the discussion in 11:1–6. Third, verse 20 tells us to be careful not to insult either the king or a rich man. This, too, can apply either to the previous discussion on politics (king) or the following discussion on wealth (rich man).

As it appears in some translations, verse 19c seems to be thoroughly cynical: "Money is the answer for everything." This is probably not a very good rendition. A better translation of the verse is, "People prepare food for pleasure, and wine makes life joyful, but money pays for both." The point is simply that people need some money to enjoy the things of this life.

ON WEALTH (11:1–6)

Ecclesiastes has devoted a great deal of space to pointing out that luxuries do not satisfy and that the quest for riches is foolish. Here, however, it gives some basic advice on maintaining one's financial health. This is not a contradiction of what has gone before. Rather, it is consistent with the Teacher's basic position that we must come to grips with what it means to be mortal.

Verses 1–2 deal with investment and not charitable giving. Verse 6 confirms the fact that this text focuses on financial strategy and not giving for compassion's sake. While charity is important and can even lead to financial security (Prov. 19:17), this is not the focus of this passage. To "cast bread upon the water" is to engage in overseas trade and make long-term investments. In other words, a person should be willing to make investments that require patience and time. To divide one's portion seven or eight ways is to diversify investments.

Verse 3 is a pair of proverbs on misfortune: "If clouds are full" (that is, if there is every sign that a storm is coming) "they pour rain upon the earth" (a storm will probably come). In other words, we should try to read economic conditions. The proverb about the tree falling is similar

Riches will never change the fact of our mortality, and they will never give true happiness. On the other hand, we should enjoy our few days under the sun and live sensibly. A stable financial life with a reasonable degree of security is important for every person.

to the English, "Whichever way the cookie crumbles"—that is, what will happen will happen. Verse 4 asserts, however, that a person can be too cautious. Those who are constantly on the lookout for storms will never get around to working and investing. The two proverbs together call us to prudence and balance. Accept the fact that things will go wrong sometimes, do the best you can to analyze the situation and make wise choices, but do not be paralyzed by caution and analysis.

In verses 5–6 the Teacher used the mystery of life to make the point that we cannot predict what God will do in the world. Thus, we can never know with certainty what enterprise will work well and what will fail. The best thing we can do is try to make sound decisions, be diligent, and be prepared for what happens.

■ *A good financial strategy is important for a*
■ *peaceful life free of excessive anxiety. One*
■ *should accept the fact that some investments*
■ *will fail. We must diversify, work hard, and*
■ *try to be careful.*

ON DEATH AND CONTENTMENT (11:7–12:7)

It is hardly surprising that the last major section of Ecclesiastes before the conclusion should focus on death. The whole book is dominated by the fact of human mortality. Here, he brings together his three themes: All is fleeting, we should enjoy life under the sun, and we should fear God.

Against those who contend that Ecclesiastes is a book of deep pessimism, the Teacher declared that "light is sweet" (11:7). He does not hate life or desire it to end. To the contrary, he wants us to enjoy all our days under the sun. He does not, however, want us to be heedless of the fact that death and "darkness" are coming (v. 8). In fact, the whole burden of this book is to help us understand that everything is *heel* so we might learn to enjoy our days in this world.

It is significant and perhaps surprising to us that the Teacher's primary exhortation is that the young man should enjoy life (11:9). When he said, "follow the impulses of your heart," NASB, he obviously did not mean to do anything you feel like doing. He did mean, however, that the young man should take advantage of the chance he has to enjoy life. He should not be so constrained or timid about life that he fails to follow a dream, take a risk, or enjoy an adventure.

The Teacher, like the book of Proverbs, addressed the "young man." This group receives special attention in Wisdom Literature because they represented the leadership for the future.

Just to make sure that no one took his advice as license to do whatever he pleased, the Teacher added, "Yet know that God will bring you to judgment for all these things." Once again, the fact that all is *heel* is a motive to enjoy life "because childhood and the prime of life are fleeting" (11:10, NASB). We do not have many days when we have the strength and freedom from responsibilities to be able to enjoy life in a carefree manner. One can almost hear the Teacher mourn for the youth who wastes these precious days either in sin or in a seriousness that allows for no joy and freedom.

The last poem of Ecclesiastes, 12:1–7, is a compelling and disturbing portrait of the decline of the body in old age. We should recall that this text is addressed especially to young people in order to encourage them to enjoy their days under the sun. It is not meant for people who are already elderly, although some may take

The Darkening of the Sun

The darkening of the sun, stars, and moon (12:2) indicates failing eyesight and possibly glaucoma. At the same time, this is an apocalyptic motif. Texts on the "day of the LORD" regularly speak of the darkening of the heavenly bodies (see Joel 3:15). In a sense, death and dying represent apocalypse for every person. As we age, the world seems to fall apart around us; when we die, the world ends.

comfort in the fact that they are not alone in struggling with the pain and inconvenience of declining health. Some interpreters have proposed very different ways of understanding this poem. For example, some say that this passage does not describe old age at all, but a funeral procession. This is unlikely. For the most part, the metaphors are descriptions of aging. Still, a funeral-like atmosphere does pervade this text.

The exhortation to "remember your Creator" (12:1) is not out of character with the rest of the passage. Throughout Ecclesiastes, fearing God is closely linked to enjoying one's days under the sun. In reality, the young man cannot really enjoy life under the sun if he does not fear God.

The "keepers of the house" that tremble (12:3) are the hands. The "strong men" that stoop are the major muscle groups of the back and legs. The "grinders" that can no longer grind because they are "few" are the teeth. "Those who look through the windows" are also the eyes, but the point here may be that the eyes have lost their sparkle.

Verse 4 describes a cruel irony. On the one hand, the "door" is closed and one cannot hear even the loud, harsh sound of grinding. In other words, deafness begins to set in. On the other hand, even the twitter of a bird is enough to wake a person up. The old person is going deaf but does not sleep well and is easily awakened.

Verse 5 mentions the fact that old people, because of their frailty, begin to be afraid of things that previously had not bothered them. They do not like ladders or stairs or even being out among strangers.

Blossoming of the Almond Tree

The blossoming of the almond tree refers to white hair.

Instead of "the grasshopper drags himself along" (NASB, NIV), this line from verse 5 should be translated, "the grasshopper becomes heavy." The point is probably that old people are physically weak and even the lightest load seems heavy. The next line of verse 5 is literally, "and the caperberry fails." This seems to refer to a loss of sexual vigor or impotence. At this point, when the whole body is failing, the individual dies, "and mourners go about the streets." The breaking of the silver cord and shattering of the golden bowl represent death; the metaphor is that these are for drawing up the water of life from a well. The return to dust (12:7) alludes to Gen. 3:19.

The Teacher's purpose is not to depress us about how bad old age is but to encourage us to enjoy the days we have and to "remember" God. A life spent without God and without joy is a waste of time.

■ *This passage is a metaphorical picture of*
■ *decline into old age. We ought to enjoy life in*
■ *the fear of God. The days when we have the*
■ *freedom to do this are very few, and the*
■ *Teacher has drawn a vivid picture of what*
■ *lies ahead in order to encourage us to make*
■ *use of the time we have.*

CONCLUSION (12:8–14)

Ecclesiastes closes by reaffirming the theme of the book that all is *heel*. By now, we should have a good understanding of what that means. It is not dour pessimism or a statement on the absurdity of life, as though the Teacher were an early twentieth-century existentialist philosopher. Instead, it is a simple assertion that we are mortal and that all the things and passions of this life are fleeting. It is a call for us to come to grips with the meaning of our mortality but in so doing to find joy and to fear God.

Many scholars believe the conclusion of Ecclesiastes was written by a later editor who was more pious than the original author. This historical reconstruction is wrong and seriously misrepresents the unified message of the whole book.

A number of interpreters take verses 8–14 to be by a later editor whom they refer to as the "epilogist" (that is, the writer of the epilogue). They have two principal reasons for drawing this conclusion. First, many interpreters believe the epilogue is much more pious than the rest of the book. Second, the epilogue speaks of the Teacher in the third person, which implies that someone other than the Teacher is speaking.

These arguments are not convincing. First, throughout the book of Ecclesiastes, the Teacher exhorted us to accept our mortality and to fear God. What is said in the epilogue is entirely consistent with the rest of the book. Second, Ecclesiastes frequently moves back and forth between first person and third person discourse. As suggested above, the *nom de plume* "Teacher" (*Qoheleth* in Hebrew or *Ecclesiastes* in Greek) is a convenient device that allows Solomon to speak about himself from a distance. By referring to the work of the Teacher in verses 9–10, the book affirms that its author devoted himself to the task of helping others learn how to cope with life.

Verse 11 says that wise sayings are like goads. This is the language of the shepherd. Good proverbs drive people in the right direction the way goads drive cattle, and all good proverbs come from "one Shepherd" (that is, God). Wise sayings are also like nails. This may refer to nails driven in the end of goads to give them sharper points, or it may switch the metaphor from driving cattle to carpentry. In other words, wise saying are like nails in that they hold a house together. It is significant that all wise teachings ultimately come from God. All truth is God's truth.

Verse 12 encourages us to maintain a balanced life. It should be translated, "Beyond all this, my son, be advised: Of making many books there is no end." To study and write too much is to spend one's life in *heel*. There is no end to it because the job of acquiring and interpreting information is never complete; we are always falling short. To seek truth is good, but we must do so without sacrificing happiness and a balanced life.

The conclusion in verse 13 should be translated, "Fear God and keep his commandments, for this is the whole of humanity." Some translations confuse the issue by adding the word "duty" and render the last line something like, "This is the duty of everyone." Others translate the last line as, "for this applies to everybody." Yet the Hebrew text actually says, very simply, "For this is the whole of humanity." In other words, fearing God and submitting to Him is the essence of what it means to be truly human.

■ *The end of the book pulls together all the*
■ *themes that make up the book of Ecclesiastes*
■ *and bring them to one, all-encompassing*
■ *conclusion: We must submit to God. To do*
■ *otherwise is to persist in a willful conceit*
■ *that refuses to come to terms with what it*
■ *means to be human.*

Verses 13 and 14 give us the conclusion of the whole book. The exhortation to fear God and keep His commandments binds together everything in the text. The fact of our mortality, our inability to control life, the emptiness of wealth, and the absurdity of politics together point to the single truth that we humans depend entirely on the mercy of God for our well-being. The exhortation to "keep his commandments" is not a call to a legalistic religion. The Teacher has already made it clear that we can never control God by our religious acts. It is, instead, a call to submission, humility, and acceptance of our lowly estate before God—a call to faith.

We were created to know, love, enjoy, and submit to God. To refuse to do this is to be something less than human. As we accept our position in the cosmos and realize that we are not little gods but are creatures of the one God, we can find the joy of being the men and women of God.

QUESTIONS TO GUIDE YOUR STUDY

1. What should be our reaction to the injustices of life?

2. What are some of the pictures the Teacher uses to describe the decline of the body?

3. What does the Teacher see as the supreme good in human life?

4. What did you find most valuable in Ecclesiastes?

SONG OF SOLOMON
INTRODUCTION

AUTHORSHIP

The title of this book is the "Song of Solomon which is of Solomon."

Today, this book goes by three names: "Song of Songs," "Song of Solomon," and (from the Latin title) "Canticles."

The date at which the book was written is widely debated, and many scholars deny that it could come from the Solomonic era in the tenth century B.C. Most of the arguments against the Solomonic authorship of Song of Solomon are similar to those used against Ecclesiastes. Many scholars believe that the language of the book resembles a late form of Hebrew. On the other hand, our knowledge of ancient Hebrew dialects is imprecise and much of the linguistic evidence is ambiguous.

Two arguments strongly support a date for this book in or around the tenth century B.C. First, Song 6:4 implies that the city of Tirzah was a rival of Jerusalem for beauty and splendor. Tirzah was in the north, and in the tenth century it was so significant that it became the first capital of the Northern Kingdom after Israel split into two kingdoms. Omri, however, who reigned from 885 to 874, made Samaria the new capital city in the north (1 Kings 16:24), and thereafter Tirzah rapidly declined into obscurity. If the Song was written in 450 B.C., when Tirzah was long forgotten, why would a poet describe it as Jerusalem's equal and use it as a metaphor for splendor?

From about 1300 to 1100 B.C., Egyptian poets produced a distinctive type of love poetry. This Egyptian literature is remarkably similar to the Song of Songs. It is impossible to deny that the Song is written in the style of this Egyptian material.

The second argument for an early date for Song of Solomon concerns the fact that in Egypt, from around 1300–1100 B.C., a type of love-poetry flourished in which a young man and a young woman declared their devotion to one another. This poetry is very similar to what we find in the Song: The Egyptian poetry and the Song use similar imagery, develop similar concerns, and use many of the same motifs. For example, both describe the man as a bounding gazelle, and both make use of the idea of "lovesickness."

The age of Solomon was chronologically not far removed from the heyday of this Egyptian love poetry, and Solomon's court had many contacts with Egypt (see 1 Kings 3:1). It is not at all surprising that someone writing love poetry at this time in Israel would make use of motifs which appeared in the Egyptian poetry. It would be unprecedented, however, if someone living in Palestine in 450 B.C. managed to reach back to an Egyptian art form more than five-hundred years old (an art form that, as far as we know, had been completely lost) and to write a poem in the very same style.

Some Bible students may be surprised, or even troubled, to discover that the Song is very similar to Egyptian love poetry. But this fact should not be disturbing. The Bible was not written in an historical vacuum. The laws of Israel have parallels in ancient law codes of Mesopotamia. The epistles of Paul have parallels in the epistolary style of the letters of the ancient Roman world. If the Bible were being written today, its books would follow contemporary style. Following the style of an ancient culture does not mean that the content is pagan or that it is not inspired by God.

MEANING

For most of us, however, the real question about Song of Solomon is what it means. Its language is strange and hard to understand, and its images are almost as bizarre as those of the book of Revelation. Who can forget Song 7:4, where the man tells the woman, "Your nose is like the tower of Lebanon"? This alone should tell us that these people used words in a way that we do not; no one would speak to the woman of his dreams in that manner today! Furthermore, readers are bewildered as they try to piece together the "story" of the Song, and they want some controlling interpretive theme that can guide them through the entire book.

In general, there are six approaches to the Song, as follows:

1. The Allegorical Interpretation

This view considers the Song an allegory of the love between God and Israel (Jewish view) or between Christ and the Church (Christian view). Beyond these two basic interpretations, there are as many different allegorical readings of the Song as there are allegorists. Some interpreters take it to be a portrayal of the history of the church or Israel, and there are countless subinterpretations. Roman Catholics tend to give the Virgin Mary a prominent position in the interpretation of the Song. Typical allegorical readings are that kisses (1:2) are the Word of God, that the woman's dark skin (1:5) represents her sin, that her breasts (7:7) are the nurturing doctrine of the church, and so forth.

One often hears the idea that the Song would not have been allowed into the Bible if it had not first been interpreted allegorically. This is certainly incorrect. It is far more likely that the

The most famous allegorical interpretation of the Song of Songs is a series of messages by Bernard of Clairvaux. He preached eighty-six sermons on the first two chapters of the Song.

The idea of allegorizing ancient books actually began among pagan Greek philosophers who were embarrassed at all the stories that told about promiscuity, petty behavior, and violence among the Olympian gods. These philosophers argued that these stories of lust and vengeance were actually allegories that concealed philosophic truth. Early in the history of the Church, a number of Christians began to believe that sexual pleasure was intrinsically evil. Not surprisingly, these Christians were scandalized at the thought of taking the Song at face value. Their solution was to adopt the same strategy that the pagan philosophers had followed in reading the myths: They read the text allegorically. They therefore argued that the only proper way to read the Song was to discern spiritual lessons concealed in the poetry. They refused to consider the possibility that it might actually be about love between a man and a woman.

Song was allegorized because it was already in the Bible, and people wanted to explain how it came to be there. If it were not in the Bible, no one would think of reading it as an allegory.

In favor of allegorizing the Song, we might argue that the New Testament sometimes calls the church the "bride of Christ." However, notice that the New Testament never allegorizes any text from the Song and that it never describes the love between Christ and the church in terms of physical sexuality (with kisses and so forth). To the contrary, we would be shocked at the idea of Christ declaring his love for the Church using terms anything like 7:7–8. In reality, the blending of spirituality and sexuality is characteristic of paganism and cults, not of biblical faith, and only a pagan deity would use such language with his devotees.

The strongest argument against reading the Song allegorically is simply that it never hints that it is an allegory. Elsewhere, when Scripture gives an allegory, it gives us very clear signs that the text is to be read allegorically (for example, Judg. 9:7–15).

2. The Dramatic Interpretation

This interpretation takes the Song as a drama that tells a complete story. Like any good play, it has a number of characters who say their lines and carry the plot forward. There are two distinct dramatic interpretations. The first, the "two-character" drama, reads the Song as the tale of how Solomon for a short time enjoyed a pure and beautiful love with one woman. The other interpretation is the "three-character" drama. It states that this is a play with three major characters. These are Solomon, a woman called the "Shulammite," and her "shepherd lover." The play tells how Solomon tried to draw her into his harem but failed because she was devoted to her rustic lover and rejected Solomon's overtures.

The fact that there are two completely different dramatic interpretations of the Song points to an obvious problem. In order to take the Song as a drama, so many details must be read into the text that two interpreters inevitably have radically different interpretations of the story line. Even among scholars who hold to a three-character interpretation, major differences of interpretation exist. Since everyone who follows a dramatic interpretation must read large amounts of information into the text, it is no surprise that they rarely agree among themselves. One can only come up with a plot line, scenes, and episodes by inventing them and forcing them on the Song.

The reality is that there is no reason to suppose that the Song is trying to tell a coherent, complete story. We have no evidence that the drama as an art form existed in ancient Israel.

3. The Historical Interpretation

This view is the same as the dramatic interpretation except that it claims that the drama described in the Song actually happened—that Solomon and the woman really did the things described in the Song. It, too, has "two-character" and "three-character" versions, and it is subject to the same problems as the dramatic interpretations. We should bear in mind that the Song never implies that it is telling a story or giving us a piece of court history.

4. The Cultic Interpretation

This analysis of the Song is popular among a few scholars. It claims that the Song actually

The first true dramatic plays we know about were the dramas from Greece in the fifth century B.C. This was long after the time of Solomon.

describes ancient fertility religion and a sacred marriage between a god and goddess. This view, too, requires that an enormous amount of detail be read into the text, and it should be rejected completely.

5. The Wedding Interpretation

This view states that the Song was the text for a wedding ceremony in ancient Israel. It has much more to support it than the other interpretations we have mentioned so far, but it has some major weaknesses as well. Although the Song obviously has something to do with marriage, it is not possible to use it to reconstruct in any convincing manner an Israelite wedding ceremony. It is more likely that the Song revolves around a wedding but is not actually the text for a wedding ceremony.

6. The Love Song Interpretation

This view states that the Song is exactly what it appears to be: a love song in three parts for a man, a woman, and a chorus of women. There is no convincing evidence for the existence of other singers, such as a second man or a chorus of the woman's brothers. Because it is a love song and not a drama or even a ballad, one should not expect to find a coherent story. It is a series of images that revolve around romantic love, expressing the emotions of fear, excitement, trauma, and joy. It explores how a young couple in love feels and gives expression to the emotions of this magical time of life. This is the most natural approach to the Song.

Love songs by nature give only the bare outlines of a story without including many specific details or following any kind of plot development. For example, many love songs basically convey the message, "I love you. Why did you leave me?" From that, the listener realizes that a love relationship has broken down and learns a few other details, but he or she does not hear a fully developed narrative. Song of Solomon, similarly, celebrates the consummation of love between a man and woman without giving a full history of their romance.

This book extols the coming together of a bride and groom for their first night of love on their honeymoon. This event stands at the very center of the book (4:16–5:1), where the woman asks the man to "come into his garden" and he replies, "I have come into my garden, my sister, my bride." The Song uses symbolic language to describe their excitement about their first experience with sexuality. It also expresses her anxiety over the loss of her virginity (once again using a great deal of symbolism).

When we read the Song, we should always see the language as expressions of how the man and woman feel and not as literal events. Thus, when the man says to the woman, "Your nose is like the tower of Lebanon," he does not mean that she has a gargantuan nose. He means that just as he is awestruck by the beauty and symmetry of that tower, so he is awestruck by the beauty and symmetry of her nose, eyes, neck, hair, and all of her body.

Poetic imagery from the biblical world is often very different from the kind of symbolism we know. The strange visions of Ezekiel 1 and the poetry of Song of Songs are different from one another, but both show us that the ancient Israelites could express ideas in ways that modern culture finds bizarre and confusing.

MEANING

Why is this book in the Bible and what are its lessons for us? First of all, the Bible is meant to help us through every aspect of life. Certainly, the most important issue we have to deal with is our relationship to God, but after that, few items are as important as understanding the love relationship of marriage. The Bible would be missing something important if it did not include this book.

In its celebration of love, the Song tells us that although sexual immorality is a terrible danger to a person's soul, sexuality itself is a good gift from God that is enjoyed best by those who know God. The Song promotes a proper sexual morality not by laws but by example. It states, "This is the joy that awaits those who wait and who love God. This—not adultery, promiscuity, homosexuality, or bigamy—is the way to discover the true meaning of sexual love."

Second, the Song is a needed corrective to the ascetic tendency that often appears in the church. This is the view that the world and the body are innately evil and that any form of pleasure is degrading. In effect, this view finally asserts that creation itself is a bad thing, contrary to Gen. 1. The Gnostics, an early Christian heresy, took this path.

Third, the Song separates sexuality from spirituality. Each has its proper sphere, but we should not mix the two. Pagan cults made the sex act into a ritual of worshiping the gods. In the Song, love between a woman and a man is a beautiful thing under God, but it is not a part of worship. It is part of our life "under the sun."

Finally, this book is an expression of the grace of God. Legalism, frightened of the power of sexuality, wants to hide it, deny that it exists, and try to smother it. Grace says, "Yes, you are a sinful people, and you must be careful to use God's gifts in the right way. But you will never learn to do this by running away from life. God will give you the power to live life in the right way."

OUTLINE

Like Ecclesiastes, Song of Solomon does not follow a traditional, point-by-point outline. Few love songs ever do! Instead, it gives us the lyrics that the various singers are to sing. There are lyrics for the lead female singer, lyrics for the lead male singer, and lyrics for the chorus. Put another way, Song of Solomon is not the script of a play; it is the libretto for a musical performance. It is sometimes difficult to tell which singer sings which part, but below is a reasonable reconstruction:

Title (1:1)	Woman (1:2–4a)	Chorus (1:4b)
Woman (1:4c–7)	Chorus (1:8)	Man (1:9–11)
Woman (1:12–14)	Man (1:15)	Woman (1:16)
Man (1:17)	Woman (2:1)	Man (2:2)
Woman (2:3–10a)	Man (2:10b–15)	Woman (2:16–3:5)
Chorus (3:6–11)	Man (4:1–15)	Woman (4:16)
Man (5:1a, b)	Woman (5:2–8)	Chorus (5:9)
Woman (5:10–16)	Chorus (6:1)	Woman (6:2–3)
Man (6:4–9)	Chorus (6:10)	Woman (6:11–12)
Chorus (6:13a)	Man (6:13b–7:9a)	Woman (7:9b–8:4)
Chorus (8:5a)	Woman (8:5b–7)	Chorus (8:8–9)
Woman (8:10–12)	Man (8:13)	Woman (8:14)

We should add that the Song does have internal structure. The second half of the Song mirrors the first half in reverse order (a chiastic structure). For example, in 1:5–7 and again in 8:10–12, the woman sings of her work in her vineyard. In 2:16–17 and 6:2–3, we have the refrain, "My lover is mine." At the very center of the book, the woman invites the man to enter "his garden" (speaking of herself) and he declares that he has entered it (4:16–5:1a).

■ *The whole Song revolves around the first*
■ *sexual union of a married couple.*

SONG OF SOLOMON COMMENTARY

Superscript

Above many psalms in the English Bible is a small note indicating something about the authorship or historical circumstances of the psalm or giving some kind of musical information (e.g., "with stringed instruments"). These notes are part of the Hebrew Bible, and in the Hebrew versification, they actually form the first verse of a psalm. These were written by scribes who lived during the Old Testament period.

TITLE (1:1)

Like the superscripts to many psalms, this verse gives the background information on the song that follows it. Unlike some superscripts, however, it gives no information about the occasion when this song was written. By contrast, the superscript of Ps. 57 says that it was written when David "fled from Saul into the cave." The superscript to Song of Solomon only says that it is the best song (for that is what "song of songs" really means) that belongs to Solomon. In indicating that the Song of Solomon is "Solomon's," the text may mean that it was by Solomon or that it belongs in the Solomonic collection and was perhaps a composition of one of his court musicians.

WOMAN (1:2–4a)

The woman opened with a call for the man to come and give her his love. His kisses are like wine, a simile that may refer to the taste of his kisses or to their intoxicating effect on her. It is important to see that she shifted easily from talking in the third person about him ("let him kiss me") to speaking directly to him ("for your love is better than wine)." This freedom of movement between second and third person sometimes makes it difficult to tell whether there is a change of speaker.

The end of verse 2 and the beginning of verse 3 are joined together and should be translated as follows: "For your love is better than wine; it is better than the fragrance of your perfume." His love excites her senses and she feels that other

In many societies where women frequently must work outside and normally have tanned skin, fair skin is regarded as especially attractive. Darker skin would be a sign that a person belonged to the peasant class.

When she says that she is beautiful although dark, we need to realize that she reflects the outlook of an agricultural economy in which people tended to regard fair skin as more attractive than dark skin. In a world in which most women worked in the fields, dark skin would have been common, and people generally regard the exotic or unusual as attractive. Centuries ago, artists portrayed beautiful women as very pale; in some cultures women wore white makeup.

women envy her ("therefore, the women love you"). When she calls him the king, she is using the language of love. Her call for him to take her away to his chambers perhaps reflects her desire for the wedding night.

CHORUS (1:4b)

The plural "we" in "We will exult and rejoice in you; we will praise your love more than wine" (NRSV) implies that the chorus is singing. They are echoing what the woman has sung, and the effect is to reinforce her words.

WOMAN (1:4c–7)

The woman responded by declaring that "rightly" the women love him. In effect, she is saying that everyone can see what a wonderful man he is.

The woman then turned to herself and felt the need to defend herself. She is "dark" but beautiful. This is not a racial statement, and it should not be used to justify opinions on racial matters.

In verse 4 she called her beloved a "king," but now she describes him as a "shepherd" who must give his flocks rest at midday. Since she described herself as a peasant, it is likely that he was a shepherd instead of a king.

CHORUS (1:8)

This line is often taken to be the man's response to her query. It is odd, however, that he would give such imprecise directions. It could be that he was teasing her. It seems better, however, to read this as an exhortation from the chorus to her: if you want to find your man, go where he may be found, among the sheep! Perhaps the point is that a woman should not hesitate to go find the man she loves.

MAN (1:9–11)

The man is not saying that she looks like a horse! A mare harnessed to Pharaoh's chariot would be adorned in costly and decorative ornamentation and would have been a glorious, impressive sight. In the same way, the sight of her leaves him awestruck. He called her a mare obviously because she was a woman; the point is not that Pharaoh's chariots were drawn by mares.

It is interesting that he said that he would make her golden earrings (v. 11). Presumably, such jewelry was beyond the means of the average shepherd and would not have been worn by a peasant woman. Again, however, this is the language of love. When he spoke of giving her expensive jewelry, he declared how much he valued her and how he wanted to give her the best.

WOMAN (1:12–14)

Here, the woman spoke of her lover as (1) a king, (2) a sachet of myrrh, and (3) henna blossoms. It is no more necessary to take the first literally—that he is a king—than it is to take the second and third literally. All of these are expressions of how much she loved him.

MAN (1:15)

The man's declaration of admiration is elegant in its simplicity. It is not entirely clear, however, in what sense her eyes are "doves." It may be that they appear tranquil, much as the cooing of a dove gives a feeling of serenity.

WOMAN (1:16)

The woman responded to the man in kind except that where he called her eyes "doves," she spoke of their bed as "green" like the boughs

Egyptian art depicts the chariots and horses of the Egyptian kings. They are decorated with splendid colors to give them a regal appearance.

"Sachet of Myrrh"

Verse 13 could well be rendered, "A sachet of myrrh is my lover to me; between my breasts he will sleep." He is like a sachet of myrrh in that she will enjoy the fragrance he gives (an idea that is probably both literal—the smell of his body after it has been anointed with oils—and metaphorical—the love he gives her). The metaphor of him being between her breasts like a sachet of myrrh is arresting. The Bible elsewhere speaks of a woman's breasts as a special place of love between man and woman (Prov. 5:19).

Humility is an important quality to look for when seeking a spouse. Someone who is selfish and narcissistic will not be able to love, bear setbacks, or forgive.

The precise botanical identities of these flowers are uncertain. They are not necessarily the modern, English namesakes of these flowers.

The apple tree is superior to the other trees in that it bears large, conspicuous, and edible fruit. Some scholars suggest that the Hebrew word here refers to the apricot, but the interpretation as "apple" is still preferable. Fruit, in the Song, often metaphorically describes sexual attributes, and it most often appears in descriptions of the woman. Here, however, the woman describes the man as pleasurable to her in the metaphors of shade and fruit.

of a tree or a field of thick grass. Greenery, like pastoral settings, often finds its way into romantic poetry and song.

MAN (1:17)

This line could be taken to be the woman's, but since it appears that they are singing antiphonally at this point, it is best to ascribe this to the man. What he describes is not an actual house but a romanticized love nest.

WOMAN (2:1)

The woman is not boasting in calling herself "the rose of Sharon" and the "lily of the valleys." She is actually being very modest and simply saying that she is one of many young girls whom the man could have chosen. She is saying, "I am just a common flower of the field."

MAN (2:2)

The man's response corrected her (in his eyes) excessively humble self-evaluation. She is not just one among many flowers; she is a flower among thorns! Thus he regarded her as surpassing in every way the beauty and grace of all other young women.

WOMAN (2:3–10a)

In verse 3a, the woman returned the man's compliment with a compliment in kind. As she is a flower among thorns, he is an apple tree among the other trees.

The "banquet hall" in verse 4 (NIV) is literally the "house of wine." In all probability, however, the "house of wine" is a metaphor for the man's love having an intoxicating effect on her. She has just spoken of him as an "apple tree" (v. 3), and in verse 6 she says that she is in his arms.

In verse 5 she declares that she needs to be sustained with raisins and apples; she is lovesick. In the Egyptian love poetry, the singers often describe themselves as sick from their yearning for love. Here again, the fruit she longed for may not be literal fruit but her beloved.

One cannot help but wonder what is meant by the woman's calling on the Jerusalem girls, the chorus, by the "gazelles and does of the field." Some take this expression to be a code word for the divine name "God Almighty," since the Hebrew for "gazelles" and "does" looks like the Hebrew for "God Almighty." However, in Song of Solomon, gazelles represent youth, beauty, and sexual vigor. She seems to be making word-play in using words that sound like "God Almighty," and yet she has her friends make an oath by something far different, gazelles and does. The point of the oath is that the young women should not spend their youth and sexual vigor foolishly. She tells them "not to awaken love until it desires."

Having called on the chorus to swear an oath by the gazelle, the woman suddenly exclaimed that she sees her beloved coming, leaping over the hills like a stag (v. 8). To her he is virile, handsome, and attractive. The metaphor changes when he comes and looks in at her window—something that the stags in ancient Israel probably rarely did. But his looking in at the window is an invitation for her to become a doe and join him. The leaping of the gazelle on the hills represents the physical play that he wants her to join him in. Then, she says, he spoke to her.

MAN (2:10b–15)

This song is an invitation for the woman to come away with the man. It is presented in a

"His banner over me is love"

The expression, "his banner over me is love" in verse 4 is very popular, but it is not certain that this is what the Hebrew actually means. It may mean, "His intention for me is love." This translation is less poetic but easier to understand.

The idea is that a person should not enter into sexual activity until the proper time. One should not spend sexual energy on experimentation and youthful infatuation. Sex is powerful and can be a delight, but it needs to be held in check until the right time and the right person comes along. The Song does not explicitly speak of marriage here. Nevertheless, it is not a great leap from what the text explicitly asserts to say that a person should refrain from sex until marriage and refrain from marriage until he or she is prepared and capable of making a mature decision. See 1 Thess. 4:3–5.

The Hebrew poets often used full descriptions of places and things in order to paint a complete picture. When Ps. 23 says that God makes His sheep lie down in "green pastures," the text obviously means that these are good pastures that are full of food and pleasant to lie in. Beyond that, however, the color *green* has no special symbolic significance. One should be careful about letting the imagination run free in seeking an interpretation of a text.

The woman called on her lover to be like a gazelle on the "mountains of Bether." Scholars debate over the meaning of the "mountains of Bether." The NIV translates this inaccurately as "rugged hills." If "mountains of Bether" is to be translated at all, it probably means "split mountains." Whether there really was a place called "split mountains" in ancient Israel (which is very doubtful), she probably referred to her breasts. It was there that she wants her beloved to browse like a gazelle.

beautiful and pastoral announcement of the arrival of springtime. The winter is over, the flowers are in bloom, and the trees have their early fruit. There is a fairly universal association between springtime and the feelings of love and romance. The call to come away with him is an invitation to love. Flowers and fruit also imply fertility.

Verse 15 is very difficult to interpret, and an almost endless variety of sexual and theological ideas have been read into it. What are the "little foxes," and why does he want her to come catch them?

Chasing little foxes out of the vineyards of ancient Israel in springtime was probably a necessary duty but also an activity that children and young people made into a game. The man's invitation need mean nothing more than that he was calling her to come out and "play" in the manner that young couples in love often do.

WOMAN (2:16–3:5)

The woman picked up her song where she had left off, describing the man as a stag. Both singers have referred to the woman as a "lily" (2:1–2), so it seems clear that the lilies refer to the pleasures of the woman.

The tone of the woman's song abruptly changes at 3:1. From a call for her lover to browse among the lilies on the "split mountains," she suddenly shifted to a strange nighttime episode. She told of lying awake deep into the night on her bed while she awaited her beloved. She then got up to seek him in the streets and asked the night watchmen if they had seen him. Immediately she found him, held him, and took him to her "mother's room." Following this, she repeated her charge to the women of Jerusalem not to awaken love. This episode has a close parallel in 5:2–8. It is a severe challenge to interpreters.

One can group the interpretations of this sequence into four categories: the literal, the cultic, the dream, and the symbolic. If taken literally, this means that the young woman had two very similar experiences—that she wandered the streets in search of her lover in order to take him to her mother's house, and that on one occasion she was beaten by guards.

While at first glance this might appear plausible, on close inspection· it is highly unlikely. A woman who searched the streets in this way would probably be a prostitute (Prov. 7:10; Hos. 2:7). It is unlikely that a young man would be taken to the home of his girlfriend's mother for a sexual encounter unless, again, the woman were some kind of prostitute (in ancient Israel a bride was taken into her husband's household). Furthermore, a love song in which the woman gets beaten and stripped by guards is quite bizarre if taken literally.

The "cultic" interpretation takes the myth of Baal and Anat as its starting point. In this myth, the goddess Anat seeks the body of Baal after he has been slain by the god Mot. Nothing in the Song supports linking the myth to this text.

The "dream" interpretation is really not an interpretation at all but the avoidance of having to interpret the episode. Anything can happen in a dream, of course, so there is no need to explain the meaning of events if it is only a dream. Nothing in the text indicates that this is a dream.

The "symbolic" interpretation asserts that this is part of a song and not a biography, myth, or

In the Ugaritic myth of Baal and Anat, the god Baal is slain by the god Mot. Baal's consort Anat then goes in search of him. Some people see a parallel between Anat's search for Baal and the woman's search for her beloved in the Song, but the similarity is probably coincidental.

dream. As such, it needs to be interpreted and not simply taken literally or dismissed as unreal. We must answer the hard questions of why she could not find her lover, why she roamed the streets, why she met guards, and what she meant by taking him to her mother's house.

The fact that the woman spoke of herself as alone on her bed implies that this part of the Song concerns her inner, private thoughts. Furthermore, she seems to be anticipating her moment of love with the man. The best solution to this problem is that this text describes her anxieties over the approaching moment when she will lose her virginity.

Wandering in the streets in search of the man represents her desire to entice the man. As mentioned above, this activity is associated with the prostitute in Prov. 7:10–13, although Lady Wisdom, a symbolic counterpart to the prostitute, does the same (Prov. 1:20–21). Again, the woman did not literally wander the streets seeking her man; this is simply a motif that represents her desire to entice him.

The guardians of the city symbolize her virginity. Elsewhere, the book describes the woman herself as like a city (6:4). Virginity prior to marriage was of utmost importance in ancient Israel, and the loss of virginity was the great transition in a woman's life. A woman's virginity was itself the guardian of her chastity; as long as her virginity was intact, she was relatively inaccessible to young men. When Amnon lusted for Tamar, the Bible tells us, "it seemed impossible" for him to do anything to her because she was "a virgin" (2 Sam. 13:2).

As she longed for her beloved, the "guards" who "circle the city" suddenly came upon her. In other words, as she longed for her beloved, she also struggled with the issue of her own virginity. It is also noteworthy that she asked the guards where her lover was; her virginity was the key to her obtaining her lover, just as ancient Israelite society demanded that a young bride be a virgin.

She then seized him and was determined to take him to "her mother's house." The "mother's house" is probably a euphemism for her own sexual organs. That is, her "mother's house" is the womb, the place where she was conceived. As her mother took in her father, so she now is determined to take in her beloved. In short, this text concerns the anxieties of a young woman as she struggled with the pull of her love for her man and her equally strong fear over losing her virginity.

Thus, it is not surprising that she again called upon the girls of Jerusalem not to "awaken love" until the proper time. Although frightening, the moment of giving up her virginity was also highly meaningful, and she warned the other girls not to hasten into it.

CHORUS (3:6–11)

The text gives no clear indication of who is the singer of this part, but it seems unlikely that the woman has abruptly gone from her dramatic account of 3:1–5 into this announcement of "Solomon's" arrival. Certainly the man is not the singer. It appears that the chorus is the best candidate, although one might challenge this on the grounds that they call on the Jerusalem girls to come out and see "Solomon" (v. 11). However, there is no reason to suppose that the chorus is supposed to be all the girls of Jerusalem. It is

The name *Solomon* connotes regal splendor. We see this even in the New Testament, where Jesus used Solomon as a representative of all the glory that wealth can give (Matt. 6:29).

likely that the chorus is calling on other Jerusalem girls to come.

The description of the arrival takes on some of the character of a theophany (an appearance of God). There is a column of smoke, much like the column of cloud that accompanied Israel in the desert (Exod. 13:21–22). The myrrh and incense are reminders of the incense that burned in the Temple (Exod. 30:1–9). This does not mean that the text is describing a true theophany; it is merely using language that would suggest splendor and glory to its ancient readers. They declared that it was "Solomon's carriage" with his accompanying warriors.

This does not mean, however, that the historical Solomon is a "character" in the Song. Instead, "Solomon" is a figure of regal glory, much as we might declare that a physically strong man is a real "Hercules." Even in Jesus' day, the name of Solomon was synonymous with regal splendor (Matt. 6:29). It is probable that this was a figure meant to convey the coming of a bridegroom for his bride. On this festive occasion, the bridegroom would be dressed in the finest clothes available and would be in every sense a "king" for that day. The "sixty warriors" is probably an equally grand way of describing the "friends of the bridegroom," or "the groomsmen," as we would call them. Their function of fending off the "terrors of the night" is purely symbolic.

We do not know details of the wedding customs of this time, but it is possible that the groom was carried in on a sedan chair (v. 10). It is probably important that this account of the arrival of the groom comes immediately after the woman's anguished struggle over the loss of her virginity in 3:1–5. As soon as she has declared her intent to take her lover to her "mother's house," we are ushered into a wedding scene.

MAN (4:1–15)

This passage is the longest of the man's parts. It comes immediately after the woman's wrestling with her thoughts about losing her virginity (3:1–5), and the choral announcement of the arrival of the groom in 3:6–11. This is followed by two verses that can only be taken as the consummation of the marriage of the man and woman (4:16–5:1). Therefore, the man's song in 4:1–15 is best interpreted as a song of tender wooing, appropriate as an expression of a man's love for his bride as he approaches her on their wedding night.

This interpretation is supported by the fact that he praised her for the beauty of her body and mentioned parts of the body that would normally be covered (the breasts, v. 5). In fact, it is interesting that he began by speaking of her eyes "behind a veil" (v. 1) but moved to describing intimate parts of her body and declared that her body has no flaw (v. 7).

He began by speaking of her eyes as "doves" (v. 1), which either means that they are gentle or that they communicate tenderness, like the cooing of doves. He then declared that her hair is like a flock of goats skipping down Mount Gilead. This implies vitality and grace. Her hair conveys the message that she is full of life and that there is nothing clumsy about her. In verse 2, the obvious message is that her teeth are white and none is missing. There is more here, however, than the fact that she has all her teeth! Twin lambs coming up from washing gives us a picture of youth and purity.

The full red color of her lips (v. 3) is physically beautiful. More than that, the fact that her cheeks (rather than "temples") are like pomegranates probably means more than that they have a rosy glow; it also means that they are desirable to kiss.

The comparison between her neck and the "tower of David" (v. 4) is perhaps for modern readers the strangest line yet. No visual similarity is implied beyond the obvious similarity

Ancient Israelite poetry is different than our poetic styles. Our poetry, in fact, tends to be very literal. We expect a simile to give a simple and obvious depiction of the nature of what it describes. This will not work here, where the Song describes more of how the woman makes the man feel than what the woman really looks like.

The young man has an almost reverential awe for his bride's body. A man of noble character never regards his wife's body cheaply, as though receiving the gifts she brings is nothing special.

between a neck and a tower, although it is possible that the "shields" have an analogy in a necklace she is wearing. What is especially surprising is that he describes her in military terms (tower and shields). The point may be that he feels that great dignity and strength are present in her beauty.

Obviously the woman's breasts do not look like fawns; the only literal similarity between the breasts and fawns are that there are two of each (v. 5). The simile expresses feelings of beauty, symmetry, and vitality.

In verse 6, the man abruptly broke off his praise of the woman's body and declared his intent toward her. Simply put, he wanted to spend the entire night ("until day breaks") at "Myrrh Mountain" and "Incense Hill." One hardly need make the point that these are not the names of literal hills in the area. It is probably not coincidental that he declared his desire to spend the night at these two "hills" immediately after his praise of her breasts. He then summarized his appreciation for her with the words that she is "altogether beautiful" and "flawless" (v. 7).

Verse 8, as it appears in many translations, is misleading. It should be rendered, "Come from Lebanon, O bride, come from Lebanon! Make your way! Venture from the summit of Amana, from the summit of Senir and Hermon, from the den of lions, from the lairs of leopards!" The words "with me" are not present in the Hebrew and should not be added here. In this verse, the mountains are not her breasts but some kind of high place in which the woman resides, surrounded by lions and leopards. In short, she is in a position that he cannot get to. He will have her only if she comes down to him.

The message is that the man can have her love only if she gives it voluntarily. He is awestruck by her beauty and knows that he cannot seize it. If the woman described her virginity as a city surrounded by guards, he sees it as a mountain lair protected by wild animals. It is noteworthy that her metaphor is social; for her, virginity is part of civilization and is something she must confront. For him, her virginity is wild and exotic and completely out of his reach.

In verses 11–15, he praised her for the delights her love and her body bring to him. Here, too, we probably have an appeal for her to lavish her gifts on him. In light of verse 15, "You are a garden," it is clear that in praising her pomegranates, nard, cinnamon, myrrh, and so forth, he is describing her body and not a literal garden. At the same time, it is not necessary to try to find some symbolic meaning behind each plant, as if each represented a specific part of her body. The total effect—that her love overwhelms him as a lush, spice-laden garden overwhelms him—is what matters.

WOMAN (4:16)

The woman called upon the winds to spread her fragrances to her beloved and draw him to her. In saying, "Let my lover come into his garden and taste its choice fruits," she referred to his sexual union with her. This is the high point of the text, the consummation of their marriage.

MAN (5:1a, b)

These lines belong to the man: "I have come into my garden, my sister, my bride; I have gathered my myrrh with my spice. I have eaten my honeycomb and my honey; I have drunk my wine and my milk." The phrase "my sister" is a term of affection a man would use of his

Verse 9, in the Hebrew, could be taken to mean either "you have taken away my heart" or "you have 'heartened' me." The former would mean, "I am hopelessly in love with you." The latter would mean, "You have aroused me." Both may be intended. Verses 10–11 describe the delightful, intoxicating power of her love. She overwhelms him, and he cannot imagine anything more wonderful than her love.

Ancient people frequently associated love and sexuality with gardens and the natural world. Sometimes they took this tendency too far. The fertility cults of Baal included going to prostitutes in the sacred groves of this pagan god.

At the same time, a wedding is a community event. It is not just for the bride and groom alone. When the community comes together and joins the celebration of a wedding, they are giving their blessing to the union of the couple.

In a society such as ancient Israel that placed high value on premarital virginity, the loss of virginity was a traumatic and emotional event for a woman.

beloved at this time in the ancient Near East. The spices, wine, honey, and milk refer back to the image of the woman as a garden of delights. The lines affirm, in a delicate and beautiful manner, that the man has enjoyed sexual union with his bride.

CHORUS (5:1c)

The words "Eat, friends, drink, and be drunk with love" (NRSV) express the joy of the community in the love they have found. Some readers may be puzzled and wonder if the chorus is supposed to be with the couple on their wedding night. The answer is that this is only a song; it is not a drama or a biography. The song does not imply that a crowd of women would be standing around the couple on their honeymoon bed.

WOMAN (5:2–8)

This text is obviously the companion to 3:1–6, and the interpretations of the two stand or fall together.

In verse 2 she recalled how her beloved was calling on her to "open" to him, a plea that has fairly obvious sexual connotations. He is eager to come in and appeals to her with a string of affectionate terms ("sister," "darling," "dove," and "perfect one" NASB). The phrase that he is drenched with dew expresses the urgency of his desire.

At this point (vv. 5–6) the woman feels an intense longing for the man. The text states that her hands were dripping with myrrh, but myrrh was an extremely expensive herbal ointment, and it is hard to imagine that a woman would be so extravagant in her use of it. Probably this is a sign of her sexual excitement and desire. But the man had already withdrawn. She "sought" him and "called" to him, but he was nowhere to be found.

We naturally assume that she ran into the street, but the text does not actually say this. It only comments very abruptly that the guards beat her and took away her cloak (v. 7). Taken literally, this is a brutal and astonishing scene in a love song. As a metaphor for loss of virginity, however, it is apt. The pain and bruises inflicted by the guards reflect the physical pain associated with the loss of virginity, and the removal of the cloak or veil reflects her loss of the status of virgin.

She concluded by calling on the chorus to tell her husband that she was sick (or perhaps "injured") from love (v. 8). Again, this does not mean that a young woman would literally go out and call on her friends to go and have a talk with her new husband. In the context of the Song, this is a discreet way for the woman to communicate to the man that love has been painful. She wants someone to make him understand how she feels.

CHORUS (5:9)

The chorus responded by calling on the woman to explain why the man is so special to her. In other words, they told her to deal with the fact of her love for him. She has given herself to him and has experienced great pain in the process. The process of reconciling herself to the loss of her virginity begins with her going back to the reason she gave up her virginity to him in the first place: She loves him.

WOMAN (5:10–16)

In responding to the Jerusalem girls, the woman rediscovered her love for her new husband and so recovered from the trauma of the previous text. This text is a simple admiration song in which she describes her beloved's body. Her

The early days of a marriage can be times of painful adjustment. During these times, it is good to meditate on the good qualities of our spouses. This reminds us of why we married in the first place.

praise for him knows no bounds: He is the best among 10,000 men!

He has tanned skin, a condition more desirable in men than among women in ancient Israel. This conveys not only good looks but also vitality as well (v. 10). He has thick, black hair (v. 11); that is, he is neither gray nor bald! He, too, has eyes "like doves" (v. 12; see 4:1). It may be that "eyes like doves" is simply a stock metaphor. His cheeks and lips are like spices (v. 13). As in 4:14 and 5:5, this seems to describe the pleasure she receives from his kisses.

She also described his body with terms like "gold," "chrysolite," "ivory," "sapphires," and "marble" (vv. 14–15). One cannot gain from these words any impression of what the man looked like, and they are not intended to describe his appearance. Rather, they describe how highly she values him. It may also be that his body is taut and hard, just as ivory, marble, and jewels are very hard. Also, he obviously does not look like the cedars of Lebanon. These trees are proverbial for majesty, and he is similarly majestic. At the end (v. 16) she returned to his mouth, the source of his kisses, and declared that he is her lover and companion. The anxiety and pain of virginity were gone, and she was now free to take him to herself.

CHORUS (6:1)

It is difficult for the modern reader to bear in mind that this is a song and not a dramatic production or a history. In 5:6 the man was gone when the woman opened to him; and in 5:8 she called on the Jerusalem girls to give him a message if they should find him. Thus, when the girls in 6:1 asked her where he was, one might naturally assume that they wanted some additional information before beginning a search for him.

In fact, this text has nothing to do with a literal search. We know this because in verses 2–3, when she answered their question, she knew exactly where he was. The text really means that the girls wanted to find loves of their own. It is noteworthy that they called the woman "the most beautiful of women." She was now absolutely radiant in their eyes, and they also wanted to find "him," the loving husband, as well.

True love has a transforming power, as this text shows when it describes the radiance of the woman. As long as a man continues to give love to his wife, the radiance will always be there.

WOMAN (6:2–3)

She cannot help them because he is with her and belongs to her. He is in "his garden." At this point in the Song, there can be no doubt that the garden is not a literal garden but the woman herself. He is "browsing" (not "shepherding") among the lilies. Once again, he is a gazelle feeding on lilies, and once again this represents his making love to her. If there is any doubt about what she meant, she added, "I am my lover's and my lover is mine." The Jerusalem girls would have to seek their own husbands. It was now time for her to enjoy hers.

MAN (6:4–9)

The man reaffirmed his love for the woman with another series of declarations of her beauty and perfection. A fair amount of this song repeated his earlier song of admiration, 4:1–5. This is hardly surprising. Songs routinely repeat lyrics and use standard metaphors. There may also be a message in the repetition. His love and desire for her has not diminished now that he has had sexual union with her. This contrasts with David's depraved son Amnon, who quickly came to detest Tamar after he raped her (2 Sam. 13:15). Where there is true love and a man of noble character, a woman need not fear that he will grow bored with her.

It is significant that he compared her to Tirzah and Jerusalem. By placing the two cities side by side in this manner, the Song indicates that at the time of writing the two major cities of Israel were Jerusalem in the south and Tirzah in the north. Tirzah, however, lost its status when Omri (king of the Northern Kingdom from 885 to 874 B.C.) moved the capital to Samaria. After that, Tirzah faded and became virtually a forgotten city. It is most unlikely that a poet writing in the fifth or fourth century B.C. would have placed Tirzah alongside Jerusalem as the two great cities of Israel. This verse implies that the Song was written much earlier, at least before Omri's reign.

Omri moved the capital of Israel to Samaria around 880 B.C. (1 Kings 16:24), and from that time forward the Northern Kingdom was often simply called "Samaria." Tirzah faded into insignificance.

He asked her to avert her eyes from him. He still felt shy around her. Again, the point is that although they were now married and had consummated their love, he still was in awe of her beauty.

The radiance of the woman comes from an inner beauty. It is her love for her husband and the joy he gives her that makes others notice her. The apostle Peter urged women to cultivate the inner beauty of a gentle spirit before God (1 Pet. 3:3–4).

The queens and concubines of verses 8–9 call to mind the large harem of Solomon (1 Kings 11:3). These are women of noble birth ("queens") and great beauty ("concubines"). In mentioning them here, the Song is saying that the woman surpasses all the women of the most renowned harems, even the harem of Solomon. This is a poetic device and does not mean that the woman actually belonged to the harem. Again, this is a song and not a history.

CHORUS (6:10)

We can be fairly sure that this verse belongs to the chorus because the end of the previous verse describes how young girls, princesses, and concubines all praise the woman's beauty. It is only natural that the chorus of girls would respond with a song of praise. This verse sets up an interesting contrast between this section and the beginning of the Song. In 1:3–6, the woman described herself as dark and spoke of how the women admired her lover. Now, after the consummation of their marriage, the women described her as being fair as the moon and bright as the sun, and the man observed that women praise her.

WOMAN (6:11–12)

In verse 11, the singer described going down to see if the vineyards are in bloom. This appears to be a response to the man's invitation in 2:10–15, where he invited the woman to come see the blossoms and chase the little foxes from the vineyards. This implies that 6:11–12 was sung by the woman. The translation of verse 12 is very difficult and versions differ greatly. A reasonable rendition is: "I hardly know myself! You have set me among chariots! A prince is with me!" The point seems to be that the woman is overwhelmed by the excitement of her wedding and all that it included. The "chariots" were probably ceremonial chariots that took away the new bride and groom in a festal procession. Recall that in 3:6–11 the groom arrived in some kind of ceremonial chariot.

CHORUS (6:13a)

The chorus called for the woman to come back as she was taken away in her chariot. She was no longer one of the girls of Jerusalem; she was now a married woman and must leave their company.

MAN (6:13b–7:9a)

The second half of verse 13 does not belong to the chorus. The word for "you" is plural in Hebrew, which tells us that the man is addressing the

The name *Shulammite* has been the cause of a great deal of speculation and confusion. Some interpreters suggest that it means "woman of Shulem," but to our knowledge there was no place of that name in ancient Israel. Many interpreters link "Shulammite" to "Abishag the Shunammite" of 1 Kings 1 and 2, but "Shulammite" is not the same as "Shunammite" and the ancient versions do not support this equation. Two interpretations are possible: The word *Shulammite* may mean "perfect one" and simply be a term of endearment. On the other hand, it may be a feminine form of the word *Solomon*, implying that the woman was as splendid in the chariot as Solomon. In 3:6–11 the groom arrived on a chariot and is referred to as "Solomon."

Sometimes lovers display an inappropriate possessiveness, but there is a valid possessiveness and privacy that exists between two lovers. In appropriate possessiveness, a man seeks to protect the rights and privacy of his beloved so that she is more free to be herself.

The word in 7:1 often translated as "legs" (NIV) actually means "thighs" or even "buttocks." The comparison to jewelry means that they appear finely crafted, not that they actually look like jewels. The navel is like a cup that never runs out of wine and the waist is like a heap of wheat. The navel obviously resembles a cup, but the point of the analogy is that her body never fails to satisfy him. The comparison of breasts to fawns occurs also in 4:5 and perhaps refers to gentle beauty.

chorus. The translation of the end of verse 13 is uncertain. The NIV speaks of the "dance of Mahanaim." The NRSV has "a dance before two armies." One plausible interpretation is that it means, "Why do you stare at the Shulammite as though she were a camp dancer?" In any case, it is fairly clear that he did not want people to gawk at her.

The man then began another song of praise for the woman's beauty. The call for privacy in 6:13b prepares us for this song, because in it he described her beauty as something that he alone was to enjoy.

Interestingly, in this verse he did not use a military metaphor to describe her neck (contrast 4:4). She is no longer aloof and unattainable. The term "ivory tower" in 7:4 does not connote what it might mean to a modern reader (that is, "aloof scholarship"). It means that her neck is fair and exquisite, as if the work of a master jeweler. Her nose complements her face the way a tower or mountain adds beauty to the horizon (7:4); he does not mean that her nose is large.

At the end of this song and in fairly dramatic fashion, the man described his desire to make love to her and especially to enjoy her breasts (7:6–9a). It is dishonest to take this as a text on something other than sexual pleasure in love. The phrase translated "the fragrance of your breath" (v. 8) is odd in that it literally says, "the fragrance of your nose." There is little evidence that the word for "nose" can mean "breath." There is evidence, however, that the line might mean, "the fragrance of your nipple," which fits the context better.

WOMAN (7:9b–8:4)

The woman responded with equal passion for love. It is noteworthy that the Song of Solomon has taken us through their initial desire for one another, to the anxiety of the woman over her loss of virginity, and the painful experience of the first consummation of their love. Now that this is past, they exult in their desire for one another.

This song contains material that is by now familiar, an invitation to a pastoral setting as a thinly veiled expression of a desire to make love. What is especially important here, however, is that the woman is inviting the man to come make love. She is now married, free of the restraint of virginity, and in love. Their desire for one another is fully reciprocal.

The verbs of 8:2 are generally mistranslated. She is not saying that she wished she could take him to her "mother's house" but could not. The verbs should be rendered, "I *will* lead you to my mother's house," and "I *will* give you spiced wine" rather than, "I *would* give you spiced wine." Since she cannot give him even minimal affection openly, she will give him all her affection in private. Once again, the "mother's house" is probably more than a house (in ancient Israel a woman joined her husband's household; the husband did not move into his mother-in-law's home). The term "mother's house" is a euphemism for the female reproductive organs. She means that she will take him into herself.

As before, she exhorted the Jerusalem girls to maintain their virginity until the proper time (8:4). In the exhilaration she felt as a young wife, she told them this was worth waiting for.

It is difficult for some Christians to reconcile themselves to the fact that God really does approve of the joy they can have in a loving, sexual relationship within marriage. A lingering sense of shame makes us think that even in the right context, having sex is somehow wrong.

Mandrakes (v. 13) were regarded as an aphrodisiac (Gen. 30:14–16).

Married women can instruct unmarried women, and older women can instruct younger wives about love and marriage. Paul, in Titus 2:4, called on the older women to teach young women.

Her wish that he were her brother (8:1) is strange to modern ears. The point is not that she wanted to make love to him in broad daylight; it is simply that she wished her culture did not forbid her showing any signs of affection to him in public. She was free to kiss a family member in the open, but any show of affection toward her husband would be regarded as quasi-sexual and thus scandalous.

CHORUS (8:5a)

The first half of 8:5 has a parallel in 3:6a, where the chorus sang. Thus, it is reasonable to suppose again that this was the chorus. They appear to be watching the man and woman as they ride in a chariot, but their focus is on the woman. Again, this contrasts with the early parts of the Song, where the women of Jerusalem were dazzled by the man. Here, they looked upon the woman in a position of repose and trust with her husband.

WOMAN (8:5b–7)

The woman is again the singer (the word "you" in the Hebrew here is masculine, which implies that she, not he, is the speaker). The language again is obviously sexual. She spoke of how his mother conceived and gave birth to him. In 2:3 she called him an "apple tree."

She attested to the exclusiveness and power of love in 8:6–7. Her appeal to him to place her as a seal over his heart is perhaps a call for absolute fidelity in mind and body. This kind of love can allow for no rival.

Therefore, when she spoke of the man's mother conceiving him "under an apple tree," we should not assume that her mother-in-law literally had sex under a tree; she meant that her mother-in-law and father-in-law together conceived her husband. She is saying that she and her husband will make love and conceive children just as their parents did.

CHORUS (8:8–9)

Many readers think that the brothers of the woman sing here, but there is no text elsewhere in the song that clearly belongs to the brothers, and there is no reason to suppose that they are abruptly introduced so late in the Song. Rather, the chorus here declared their desire to see to it that their little sister remained chaste until marriage. We have argued that the doors and guardians of 3:1–5 and 5:4–6 referred to the virginity of the woman. Here, it is evident that in speaking of the little sister as a wall and a door that needs to be barricaded, the chorus means that her virginity must be preserved. Thus, the imagery of the Song is consistent.

WOMAN (8:10–12)

The woman played on the words of the chorus to describe her situation. She too was a "wall" but unlike the little sister, her breasts were its towers (that is, the woman is sexually mature in contrast to the small breasts of the little sister). Furthermore, she is at "peace" with her beloved. That is, she need not barricade herself against the man. She is not at war with a man who wants to storm the walls by force. He is, so to speak, free to enter the gates of the citadel.

The woman contrasted her situation with that of Solomon in verses 11–12. Solomon here represents extravagant wealth. In 1:6 she mentioned that her brothers forced her to tend the family vineyard. Here, Solomon has tenants work in his vineyard. In verse 12, however, she said that she now has her own vineyard to care for and to do with as she pleases. The point appears to be that both the brothers and Solomon were detached from the life of the vineyard and had others do the labor for them.

It is true that Solomon took in great profits—five times the amount of money that the actual workers took in. But this luxury came at the price of being detached from the life of the vineyard. The woman, by contrast, knew her vineyard very well. She would tend it carefully and enjoy and give out its fruit. This obviously refers to the sexual pleasures that she and her husband will share, but it means more than that. She will nurture their life and love together. Money and power cannot buy love (8:7). It requires personal involvement.

It is important that parents and other responsible people take steps to guard the sexual chastity of young people. This does not mean literally enclosing them behind walls, but it does mean giving them specific instructions and keeping them out of dangerous situations.

If a man and woman give themselves to one another, they should bind themselves to absolute faithfulness. Love is a passion and a most precious possession. The text does not imply that couples should be racked with jealousy, but it does mean that sexual love demands loyalty. It is very surprising that she should mention death and the grave in this context. On the one hand, the simile "love is as strong as death" means that both are irresistible. On the other hand, it implies that the vow of sexual fidelity is lifelong; it lasts until the grave.

MAN (8:13)

The man declared that his friends are listening to hear her voice. The Song began with the woman singing of how the women adored her beloved (1:2–3). Now she is the center of attention. She has passed through a rite of passage and has come out radiant and full of joy.

WOMAN (8:14)

She has no concern with the admiration of the men. She only calls for her beloved to come with her to the "spice-laden mountains." The man and his bride depart to their life of love.

QUESTIONS TO GUIDE YOUR STUDY

1. What is the literal meaning of the Hebrew phrase translated "song of songs?"
2. What are some approaches that have been taken to interpreting the Song of Songs?
3. What can Christians learn from the Song of Songs?
4. What event does the Song of Songs celebrate?

The following is a collection of Broadman & Holman published reference sources used for this work. They are provided here to meet the reader's need for more specific information and/or an expanded treatment of the books of Ecclesiastes and Song of Solomon. All of these works will greatly aid in the reader's study, teaching, and presentation of Ecclesiastes and Song of Solomon. The accompanying annotations can be helpful in guiding the reader to the proper resources.

Cate, Robert L. *An Introduction to the Historical Books of the Old Testament*. A survey of the books of Joshua through Esther with special attention to issues of history writing in ancient Israel.

Cate, Robert L. *An Introduction to the Old Testament and Its Study*. An introductory work presenting background information, issues related to interpretation, and summaries of each book of the Old Testament.

Dockery, David S., Kenneth A. Mathews, and Robert B. Sloan. *Foundations for Biblical Interpretation: A Complete Library of Tools and Resources*. A comprehensive introduction to matters relating to the composition and interpretation of the entire Bible. This work includes a discussion of the geographical, historical, cultural, religious, and political backgrounds of the Bible.

Farris, T. V. *Mighty to Save: A Study in Old Testament Soteriology*. A wonderful evaluation of many Old Testament passages that teach about salvation. This work makes a conscious attempt to apply Old Testament teachings to the Christian life.

Francisco, Clyde T. *Introducing the Old Testament*. Revised edition. An introductory guide to each of the books of the Old Testament. This work includes a discussion on how to interpret the Old Testament.

Garrett, Duane A. The New American Commentary, vol. 14, *Proverbs, Ecclesiastes, Song of Songs*. A theological commentary on these three books of wisdom.

Holman Bible Dictionary. An exhaustive, alphabetically arranged resource of Bible-related subjects. An excellent tool of definitions and other information on the people, places, things and events of the Bible.

Holman Bible Handbook. A summary treatment of each book of the Bible that offers outlines, commentary on key themes and sections, illustrations, charts, maps, and full-color photos. This tool also provides an accent on broader theological teachings of the Bible.

Holman Book of Biblical Charts, Maps and Reconstructions. This easy-to-use work provides numerous color charts on various matters related to Bible content and background, maps of important events, and drawings of objects, buildings, and cities mentioned in the Bible.

Johnson, L. D. Layman's Bible Book Commentary, vol. 9, *Proverbs, Ecclesiastes, Song of Solomon*. A concise commentary on these Old Testament wisdom books.

Sandy, D. Brent, and Ronald L. Giese Jr. *Cracking Old Testament Codes: A Guide to Interpreting the Literary Genres of the Old Testament*. This book is designed to make scholarly discussions available to preachers and teachers.

Smith, Ralph L. *Old Testament Theology: Its History, Method and Message*. A comprehensive treatment of various issues relating to Old Testament theology. Written for university and seminary students, ministers, and advanced lay teachers.